Global Covenant

Global Covenant

The Social Democratic Alternative
to the Washington Consensus

DAVID HELD

polity

First published in 2004 by Polity Press Ltd.

Polity Press
65 Bridge Street
Cambridge CB2 1UR, UK

Polity Press
350 Main Street
Malden, MA 02148, USA

ISBN: 0-7456-3352-8
ISBN: 0-7456-3353-6 (pb)

A catalogue record for this book is available from the British Library and has been applied for from the Library of Congress.

The publisher has used its best endeavours to ensure that the URLs for external websites referred to in this book are correct and active at the time of going to press. However, the publisher has no responsibility for the websites and can make no guarantee that a site will remain live or that the content is or will remain appropriate.

Typeset in 11 on 13pt Sabon
by Graphicraft Limited, Hong Kong
Printed and bound in Great Britain by MPG Books, Bodmin, Cornwall

For further information on Polity, visit our website: www.polity.co.uk

Contents

v

Contents

Contents

Figures, Boxes and Tables

Figures, Boxes and Tables

BOXES

TABLES

Preface

Immanuel Kant wrote over two hundred years ago that we are 'unavoidably side by side'. A violent challenge to law and justice in one place has consequences for many other places and can be experienced everywhere. While he dwelt on these matters and their implications at length, he could not have known how profound and immediate his concerns would become.

Since Kant, our mutual interconnectedness and vulnerability have grown rapidly. We no longer live, if we ever did, in a world of discrete national communities. Instead, we live in a world of what I like to call 'overlapping communities of fate' where the trajectories of countries are deeply enmeshed with each other. In our world, it is not only the violent exception that links people together across borders; the very nature of everyday problems and processes joins people in multiple ways. From the movement of ideas and cultural artefacts to the fundamental issues raised by genetic engineering, from the conditions of financial stability to environmental degradation, the fate and fortunes of each of us are thoroughly intertwined.

The story of our increasingly global order – 'globalization' – is not a singular one. Globalization is not a one-dimensional phenomenon. For example, there has been an expansion of global markets which has altered the political terrain, increasing exit options for capital of all kinds, and putting new questions about the regulation of national economies on the agendas of polities everywhere. Yet the story of globalization is not just economic: it is also one of growing aspirations for international law and justice. From the United Nations system to the European Union, from changes to the laws of war to the entrenchment of human rights, from the emergence of international environmental regimes to the foundation of the International Criminal Court, there is also another narrative being told – a narrative which seeks to reframe human activity and entrench it in law, rights and responsibilities.

Many of these developments were framed against the background of formidable threats to humankind – above all, Nazism, fascism and the Holocaust. Those involved in them affirmed the importance of universal principles, human rights and the rule of law in the face of strong temptations to simply put up the shutters and defend the position of only some countries and nations. They rejected the view of national and moral particularists that belonging to a given community limits and determines the moral worth of individuals and the nature of their freedom, and they defended the irreducible moral status of each and every person. At the centre of such thinking is the internationalist or, better, cosmopolitan view that human well-being is not defined by geographical or cultural locations, that national or ethnic or gendered boundaries should not determine the limits of rights to or responsibilities for the satisfaction of basic human needs, and that all human beings require equal moral respect and concern. The principles of equal respect, equal concern and the priority of the vital needs of all human beings are not principles for some remote utopia; they are at the centre of significant post-Second World War legal and political developments.

If 9/11 was not a defining moment in human history, it certainly was for today's generations. The terrorist attack on the World Trade Center and the Pentagon was an atrocity of extraordinary proportions. It was a crime against the United States and against humanity; a massive breach of many of the core codes of international law; and an attack on the fundamental principles of the sanctity of life, the importance of self-determination, and of human rights and equal liberty. After 9/11, the US and its allies could have decided that the most important things to do were to strengthen international law in the face of global terrorist threats, and to enhance the role of multilateral institutions. They could have decided it was important that no single group or power should act as judge, jury and executioner. They could have decided that global hotspots like the Middle East which feed global terrorism should be the core priority. They could have decided that the disjuncture between economic globalization and social justice needed more urgent attention, and they could have decided to be tough on terrorism and tough on the conditions which lead people to imagine that Al-Qaeda and similar groups are agents of justice in the modern world. But they have systematically failed to decide any of these things. In general, the world after 9/11 has become more polarized and international law weaker.

Enter the war against Iraq. Saddam Hussein was a tyrant who committed massive crimes against the Iraqi and Kurdish peoples, and countries close by. But Iraq was contained. It was no longer perceived as a threat by its immediate neighbours. The evidence of a link between Iraq and global terrorist networks was weak at best, and bordering on an absence highly embarrassing to both George W. Bush and Tony Blair. Prior to the war, the UN inspectors were doing their job. Disarmament was occurring. More time could have been granted – more time to save lives on all sides, to strengthen the international consensus, to nurture international law and to protect multilateral institutions.

The rush to war against Iraq in 2003 gave priority to a narrow security agenda which is at the heart of the new American security doctrine of unilateral and pre-emptive war. This agenda contradicts most of the core tenets of international politics and international agreements since 1945. It throws aside respect for open political negotiations among states (liberal multilateralism), as it does the core doctrine of deterrence and stable relations among major powers (the balance of power). We have to come to terms now not only with the reality that a single country enjoys military supremacy to an unprecedented extent in world history, but also with the fact that it can use that supremacy to respond unilaterally to perceived threats (which may be neither actual nor imminent), and that it will brook no rival. The Clausewitzean dictum that in matters of war and peace 'the mistakes which come from kindness are among the very worst' is actively affirmed by this doctrine.

As an agenda focused on a narrow conception of security, the new American security project displaces a much more urgent focus on a broad conception of human security, based on establishing the essential conditions for human well-being and development. The US-led coalition, in pursuing first and foremost a military response to 9/11 and a war against Iraq, chose not to prioritize the development of international rules and UN institutional arrangements; and not to emphasize the urgency of building bridges between its geoeconomic and geopolitical interests and the priorities of political and social justice, which could have helped centre attention on the full gamut of threats to humankind – physical, biological, social and environmental. Moreover, the US-led coalition chose not to address the crisis of legitimacy of international institutions. Increasingly, these institutions appear either to speak for the powerful, or to be cast aside by these very same forces if they fail to fall into line with their will. And their reputation is damaged daily by the contradiction between the huge concentration of resources and personnel seeking to restore and reshape world order after the 3,000 lives were lost on 9/11, and the failure to mobilize a sustained effort to address life's daily carnage – the death of 30,000 children under five who die of preventable diseases. Shocking though this figure is, it would be even more appalling if we built into it the loss of life from threats such as global warming, killing people through heat waves, floods and storms (Houghton, 2003).

The strategy of war against Iraq, in the context of the Bush administration's doctrine of pre-emptive war, compounds anxieties about a world order moving rapidly towards a breakdown of law, respect for political autonomy and human rights. We see what this situation looks like all too clearly in the daily life of the Middle East. The intense pattern of extrajudicial outlaw killings (organized, targeted murders) on both sides of the Israeli–Palestinian conflict returns those lands to Hobbes's state of nature: the 'warre of every one against every one' – life as 'solitary, poore, nasty, brutish and short'. Peace in areas like the Middle East has been singled out occasionally as a priority by some Western leaders, but there is little sign as yet that this is part of a broader rethinking of foreign and security policy in the Middle East, and of the role of the West in international affairs more generally. These are political choices and, like all choices, they carry a heavy burden of possibility and lost opportunity.

Some American commentators, notably Robert Kagan, have reflected on the US as a necessary Hobbesian sovereign, providing security and protection to a world in need of conflict management and conflict resolution (2003). Concomitantly, he interprets the EU as a Kantian haven of peace and economic exchange, albeit parasitic upon the Hobbesian protector. In fact, current US strategy is best perceived as *pre*-Hobbesian because it betokens a return to the state of nature. Hobbes conceived of sovereign power as justified in so far as it delivers security, safety and a 'commodious' life to its people. The US strategy does none of these things, endangering its citizens (especially abroad), further dividing and polarizing international affairs, and weakening the international institutions of peace and justice.

For those who, like myself, are not pacifists and recognize the obvious dangers posed by the new terrorist networks and rogue states, and who reject the position of the current American administration and the British government, it is urgent to confront the issues which inevitably arise in this context. The following questions need addressing: What are the connections between the economic, political and security realms in our increasingly global age? How should we mould public institutions to regulate and manage these connections? And under what conditions should legitimate coercive power be wielded, to what ends, and by whom?

In the destructive climate of the current global order, there seem to be only a few plausible answers to these questions. If one objects to the answers inspired by George W. Bush, then one has to look elsewhere. As things stand, the EU has no coherent position on these matters, and no credible defence and strategic capacity to offer at this time. And while the UN may sometimes proffer a sound vision, it certainly lacks institutional mechanisms to resolve public crises effectively.

So what compelling options are there? Or, to put the matter in terms I will use later, is there an alternative to the Washington consensus, understood here as both a specific, US designed neoliberal economic project and, more broadly, a political project which underwrites the current US administration's unilateralist ambitions.

This book seeks to answer this question by setting out an agenda for addressing some of the most pressing global problems. It does so by examining how our global order is changing; how globalization is and is not reshaping our lives; how global governance can help – and hinder – political and economic development; and how a certain set of values – social democratic values – remains indispensable to a sound and feasible agenda for global change. While the volume does not shrink from addressing the question 'What options are there?', it seeks to do so within an understanding of the changing economic and political context of world order. Wisdom suggests that there was an alternative way to respond to 9/11 and the threat of Saddam Hussein, and it is not yet too late to learn. The alternative lies in a comprehensive yet practical programme of political, social and economic reform – a new global covenant for our global age. Such a covenant would be the basis of a rule-based and justice oriented, democratic multilateral order.

In order to grasp this alternative, the changing structure of the global order has to be understood. To this end, the book is divided into three parts: economics, politics and law. In each part contemporary trends are analysed, problems confronted, and a series of detailed policies set out. The aim of the book is to focus on feasible and effective policy choices which could lead to a progressive transformation of global affairs. Against the ideologues who are wholly in favour of or hostile to globalization, this book shows how global processes can be better regulated to help deliver human development, equitable economic change, democracy and justice.

DH

Acknowledgements

This book developed out of a paper I was asked to present to the Progressive Governance conference, London, 11–13 July 2003. I would like to thank everyone at Policy Network for the initial invitation and for the support they provided in the preparation for the conference.

Many people provided invaluable criticism of earlier drafts of the conference paper. I would like to thank, in particular, Anthony Giddens, Andrew Gamble, Mary Kaldor, Mathias Koenig-Archibugi, Matt Browne, Jonathan Perraton, Jean François Rischard, Zaki Laïdi, Phillipe Legrain, David Mepham and Stephany Griffith-Jones. Phillipe Legrain and David Mepham have been particularly helpful on trade and aid reform; Stephany Griffith-Jones provided much useful guidance on the reform of international finance institutions; and Andrew Gamble, Jonathan Perraton and Mathias Koenig-Archibugi offered valuable advice about the shape of the entire work. Ed Victor helped formulate the title, and I would like to express my appreciation to him as well.

Acknowledgements of my many intellectual debts would not be complete without special mention of Anthony McGrew. He and I have worked together on studies of globalization, global governance and global politics for over a decade. Our books such as *Global Transformations, Governing Globalization* and *Globalization/Anti-Globalization* form a core part of my intellectual make-up, and little I write about today stands wholly independently of this output. Our weekly, if not daily, exchanges on diverse topics have provided an invaluable stepping stone for this book.

Acknowledgements

In addition, I would like to thank everyone at Polity – particularly John Thompson, Gill Motley, Pam Thomas and Ann Bone – for their extraordinarily professional help at all stages of production and marketing. They continue to be a home away from home!

Finally, chapters 7–9 are based on research I am doing on politics and international law with the help of a Major Research Fellowship from the Leverhulme Trust. I would like to thank the trust for their generous support, which has made this part of the book possible.

Some sections of this book have been adapted from previously published essays. The details are as follows:

'Law of states, law of peoples', *Legal Theory*, 8 (2002). Parts of this essay were adapted to form chapter 7.

'Cosmopolitanism: globalization tamed?', *Review of International Studies*, 29 (2003). An adapted version of sections of this essay forms part of chapter 5.

'Global social democracy', in A. Giddens (ed.), *The Progressive Manifesto* (Cambridge: Polity, 2003). Sections of this essay form part of the Introduction and chapters 3 and 6.

'Democratic accountability and political effectiveness from a cosmopolitan perspective', *Government and Opposition* (forthcoming 2004). A developed version of this article forms a section of chapter 6.

The author and publishers are also grateful to the following for permission to reproduce copyright material:

American Economic Review and François Bourguignon for table 3, from François Bourguignon and Christian Morrisson, 'Inequality among world citizens: 1820–1992', *American Economic Review* 92:4 (Sept. 2002);

The Economist Newspaper Ltd for box 1, drawn from 'A survey of human rights', *The Economist*, 5 December 1998;

Elsevier UK for figure 4, from B. Milanovic, 'Two faces of globalization: against globalization as we know it', *World Development* 31:4 (2003), pp. 667–83;

The European Commission for table 2, from *Making Sense of Globalization* (London: Centre for Economic Policy Research, 2002);

Foreign Policy for figure 5, from Foreign Policy Online, www.foreignpolicy.com, permission via Copyright Clearance Center;

Mathias Koenig-Archibugi for figure 8, from Mathias Koenig-Archibugi, 'Mapping global governance', in D. Held and A. G. McGrew (eds), *Governing Globalization: Power, Authority and Global Governance* (Cambridge: Polity, 2002);

Acknowledgements

Oxford University Press, Inc., for figure 3, from United Nations Development Programme, *Human Development Report 2001* (New York: Oxford University Press, 2001);

Perseus Books Group for table 1 and figure 9, both drawn from *High Noon: Twenty Global Problems, Twenty Years to Solve Them* by Jean-François Rischard (New York: Basic Books, 2002), and for box 2, from Jack Donnelly, *International Human Rights*, 2nd edn (Boulder: Westview Press, 1998), permissions via Copyright Clearance Center;

Union of International Associations for the use of data from *Yearbook of International Organizations 2001/2002* in figures 6 and 7;

United Nations Information Centre, London, for figure 2, based on data in UNCTAD, *Handbook of Statistics 2002* (Geneva: UN Conference on Trade and Development, 2002), and information in tables 4 and 5;

Professor Robert Hunter Wade for figure 1, from 'Inequality of world incomes: what should be done?', published by www.opendemocracy.net and also reproduced in Robert Hunter Wade, 'The disturbing rise in poverty and inequality', in D. Held and M. Koenig-Archibugi (eds), *Taming Globalization* (Cambridge: Polity, 2003).

Every effort has been made to trace copyright holders, but if any have been inadvertently overlooked, the publishers will be pleased to make the necessary arrangements at the first opportunity.

Abbreviations

AIDS	Acquired Immune Deficiency Syndrome
APEC	Asia-Pacific Economic Cooperation
ARF	ASEAN Regional Forum
ASEAN	Association of South East Asian Nations
BIS	Bank for International Settlements
BIT	bilateral investment agreement
CAP	Common Agricultural Policy
CBD	Convention on Biological Diversity
CEPR	Centre for Economic Policy Research
CFCs	chlorofluorocarbons
CITES	Convention on International Trade in Endangered Species
CSD	Commission on Sustainable Development
CTBTO	Comprehensive Nuclear-Test-Ban Treaty Organization (Preparatory Commission)
ECLAC	Economic Commission for Latin America and the Caribbean
EU	European Union
FAO	Food and Agriculture Organization
FATF	Financial Action Task Force
FDI	foreign direct investment
FSF	Financial Stability Forum
G5	Britain, France, Germany, Japan, USA
G7	Group of Seven (leading industrial nations): Canada, France, Germany, Italy, Japan, UK, USA
G8	Group of Eight: G7 plus Russia
G11	Group of Eleven: G7 plus Belgium, the Netherlands, Sweden, Switzerland
G20	Group of Twenty: G7 plus countries regarded as 'emerging markets'
G21	Coalition of developing countries: Argentina, Bolivia, Brazil, China, Chile, Columbia, Costa Rica, Cuba, Ecuador, Egypt,

Abbreviations

	El Salvador, Guatemala, India, Mexico, Pakistan, Paraguay, Peru, Philippines, South Africa, Thailand and Venezuela (joined latterly by Nigeria)
G77	Coalition of southern, developing countries
GATS	General Agreement on Trade in Services
GC	Global Compact
GDP	gross domestic product
GEF	Global Environment Forum
GINs	Global Issues Networks
GNP	gross national product
HIPC	highly indebted poor country
HIV	human immune deficiency virus
IAEA	International Atomic Energy Agency
IASB	International Accounting Standards Board
ICAO	International Civil Aviation Organization
ICC	International Criminal Court
ICISS	International Commission on Intervention and State Sovereignty
ICJ	International Court of Justice
IFI	international financial institution
IGO	intergovernmental organization
ILO	International Labour Organization
IMF	International Monetary Fund
IMO	International Maritime Organization
INGO	international non-governmental organization
IOSCO	International Organization of Security Commissions
IT	information technology
ITU	International Telecommunication Union
LDC	less developed countries
MARPOL	Marine Pollution convention
MEA	major economic area
MERCOSUR	Southern Cone Common Market (Latin America)
MNC	multinational corporation
NAFTA	North American Free Trade Agreement
NGO	non-governmental organization
NIC	newly industrializing countries
OECD	Organization for Economic Cooperation and Development
OPCW	Organization for the Prohibition of Chemical Weapons
PBEC	Pacific Basin Economic Council
PPP	purchasing power parity
SIPRI	Stockholm International Peace Research Institute
TRIPS	Agreement on Trade-Related Aspects of Intellectual Property Rights
UIA	Union of International Associations
UN	United Nations

Abbreviations

UNAIDS	Joint UN Programme on HIV/AIDS
UNCLOS	UN Convention on the Law of the Sea
UNCTAD	UN Conference on Trade and Development
UNCTC	UN Centre on Transnational Corporations
UNDCP	UN Drug Control Programme
UNDP	UN Development Programme
UNEP	UN Environment Programme
UNESCO	UN Educational, Scientific and Cultural Organization
UNFCCC	UN Framework Convention on Climate Change
UNICRI	UN Interregional Crime and Justice Research Institute
UNIDO	UN Industrial Development Organization
UPU	Universal Postal Union
WHO	World Health Organization
WIPO	World Intellectual Property Organization
WMD	weapons of mass destruction
WTO	World Trade Organization

Introduction

Globalization, at its simplest, refers to a shift or transformation in the scale of human organization that links distant communities and expands the reach of power relations across the world's regions. This shift can be mapped by examining the expanding scale, growing magnitude, speeding up and deepening impact of transcontinental flows and patterns of social interaction. While globalization generates dense patterns of transborder activities and networks – economic, political, legal, social, environmental, among others – it does not necessarily prefigure the emergence of a harmonious world society or a process of integration among nations and cultures. For not only does the awareness of growing interconnectedness create new forms of understanding, it also fuels deep animosities and conflicts. Since a substantial proportion of the world's population is largely excluded from the benefits of globalization, it can be a deeply divisive phenomenon. The unevenness of globalization ensures it is far from a universal process experienced uniformly across all countries.

The contest over globalization

'Globalization' is a highly contested notion. In academic discourse, whether in economics, political science or law, globalization is an intensely disputed subject and researchers do not agree on many aspects of its underlying form or trajectory. Globalization is fought over both in academia and, more broadly, in the streets from

Seattle to Geneva, Rio to Cancún. In the last few years mass protests have confronted the summits of all the major global and regional organizations, including those of the World Bank, the International Monetary Fund (IMF), the G8 (the G7 plus Russia), the European Union and APEC (Asia-Pacific Economic Cooperation). These have often been led by what has been called the global anti-capitalist or the anti-globalization movement. Representing a diverse range of social groups and non-governmental organizations, from anarchists to environmentalists, this movement has evolved as a powerful reaction against what is perceived as corporate-driven and state-promoted globalization. Beyond mass protest, single-issue campaigns, including Jubilee 2000, seeking debt cancellation for the poorest countries, and the campaign against the Multilateral Agreement on Investment, have been relatively successful in influencing the global agenda.

One of the reasons for the highly contested nature of globalization lies in the changing structure of world communications. Among the deep drivers of globalization are changes in the global communications industries linked to the revolution in information technology. The new systems of communication and information processing have helped to reconstitute not just the nature of global economic activity, but also the business of politics itself. What happens in one part of the world is readily communicated to another, and vice versa; the new communication systems can fuel reaction and counter-reaction. Yet part of the reason for the intensity of the debate about globalization lies in poignant aspects of its past. Peoples in different cultures, countries and regions have different historical experiences of globalization and different historical memories. It needs to be emphasized that there is nothing new about globalization *per se*. There have been many phases of globalization over the last two millennia, including the development of world religions, the Age of Discovery, and the spread of empires. As European countries exploded onto the world over 500 years ago, linking together parts of it that had previously been isolated, they brought with them not just new technologies and economic techniques, but also new forms of political oppression and exploitation. These early forms of globalization generated experiences and memories not just of the opportunities posed by a globally interconnected world, but of the dangers and threats. In many parts of the world this legacy continues and still conditions how contemporary forms of globalization are understood, contested and shaped.

Thus, while globalization generates increasing interconnectedness, it does not automatically generate a common set of experiences, views or values. The relation between globalization and social integration has been and remains a problematic one. This book focuses on this relation and seeks to unfold a programme – a programme I call global social democracy – which might help weave together the processes of globalization, the bonds of social integration, and the priorities of social solidarity and justice. Only a new global covenant, I argue, based on global social democracy, can succeed in developing these links.

In order to cut through the many controversies that surround the great globalization debate, it is useful to begin by dispensing with some of the most popular myths about globalization, and to highlight some of its deep drivers and challenges. The relation between globalization and social democracy will then be introduced, and the tensions between these forces examined. Following this, the book will explore three core domains at the heart of contemporary global change: economics, politics and law. The final part of the book will draw together the strands of the argument and unfold the basis of a new global compact which could link the economic processes of globalization with the core concerns of social integration and social justice.

Countering myths about globalization

While many researchers do not agree among themselves about how to characterize the main substantive processes of globalization and their impacts, there is some measure of agreement, in the light of recent research, about what globalization does not entail. Clarifying these points helps clear the ground for the main arguments that follow.

Introduction

(1) Globalization does not equal Americanization. Globalization cannot be taken as a synonym for Americanization or for Western imperialism. While it certainly is the case that the discourse of globalization, and aspects of its core processes, serve the interests of powerful economic and social forces in the West, globalization is an expression of deeper structural changes in the scale of modern social organization. Such changes are evident in, among other developments, the growth of a world trading system, the emergence of modern communication systems, the development of international law and regulation, and global environmental transformations. The US has been and remains a, if not the, key player in shaping the nature and form of economic globalization (especially of the world's current trading and financial regimes, ensuring that they commonly operate on terms favourable to its interests), but it needs to be borne in mind that American companies account, for example, for only around one-fifth of world total imports, and about one-quarter of total exports (Moore, 2003, p. 20). Globalization is not just an American phenomenon.

(2) There has been no simple race to the bottom in welfare and labour standards. A cursory survey of European countries over the last twenty years reveals that, despite experiencing many common processes of global economic change, their welfare regimes remain diverse. European welfare institutions have not converged on one single model. Their diversity testifies to the enduring significance of national state formations and national political traditions, and the importance of particular cultural and local conditions. The absence of a race to the bottom highlights the continuing significance of political institutions. Political institutions matter, and can broker different kinds of agreements between leading economic and social actors. Moreover, robust domestic institutions can play a crucial role in managing the distributive consequences of globalization. States with universal social protection, inclusive electoral representation (proportional representation), strong traditions of trade union mobilization and centralized wage bargaining have been able to mitigate the potential negative effects of international capital mobility, and, in some cases, expand the size of the public economy (Swank, 2001,

2002a).[1] Global markets do not punish developed welfare states for just maintaining high levels of social protection (Garrett, 1998; Lijphart, 1999, pp. 263–70). While developing countries are in general much more vulnerable to global economic change, and can afford less social protection, the diversity of welfare regimes in these countries also indicates the significant role played by political institutions and sound public policy in the determination of welfare and labour outcomes. These regimes are particularly fragile, however, if, like their counterparts in the developed world, they remain unembedded in a wider framework of national traditions and institutions (Rundra, 2002).

(3) There has not been a simple collapse of environmental standards. There is little question that many pressing environmental problems remain to be solved and that these are often the result of externalities generated by corporations and particular countries in their single-minded pursuit of economic growth and particular patterns of energy usage. To the extent that globalization is a spur to economic growth, and to the extent that economic growth means that countries use increasing quantities of resources and generate pollutants of diverse kinds, then globalization can be directly linked to the generation of processes that can harm the environment. As one recent report put it, while 'there is no evidence that, in general, globalization is bad for the environment ... to the extent that it improves the prospects for economic growth, globalization certainly increases the urgency of insuring that this growth is compatible with stewardship of the world's environmental resources' (CEPR, 2002, p. 106). While the last few decades have seen a growing array of new environmental standards, promulgated locally, nationally, regionally and globally, it is clear that many pressing environmental problems, such as

---

[1] Concomitantly, it has been found that where corporatist and electorally inclusive institutions are weak, and where public authority is fragmented or dispersed, international capital mobility 'is associated with downward pressures on the public economy, social transfers, and public consumption' (Swank, 2001, p. 154). Canada, the United States and Australia, among others, fit into this pattern, and have experienced market-oriented policy reforms and marked budget pressures.

global warming, will continue unabated unless the economic processes of globalization are better managed and regulated. This is a political and ethical issue as much as one about globalization *per se*. Different countries have created very different capacities in this field.

(4) Globalization is not associated with the end of the nation-state. Many have argued, or asserted, that globalization involves, or will involve, the end of the nation-state. In the first instance, the number of internationally recognized states has more than doubled between 1945 and the late 1990s to over 190 today. The high point of the modern nation-state system seems to have been reached at the end of the twentieth century, supported and buttressed by the spread of new multilateral forms of international coordination and cooperation, international organizations like the UN, and new international regimes, such as the human rights regime. The reassertion of American military power after 9/11 also highlights the extent to which powerful states can act to sustain their position and pursue their national interest. In many aspects of politics and military affairs, states remain the primary actors in world affairs. To the extent that other actors have an impact on global political and economic conditions, this tends to occur within a framework still formed and dominated by states. States matter – and world order is still shaped decisively by powerful states. None of this is to say that globalization has not altered the nature and form of political power – it certainly has. But it has not simply eroded or undermined the power of states; rather it has reshaped and reconfigured it. This leads to a much more complex political picture than the view that globalization engenders the death of the modern state.

(5) Globalization does not merely threaten national cultures. It is a mistake to confuse the globalization of communications with the globalization of culture. There is little doubt that the accelerating diffusion of radio, television, the internet and satellite and digital technologies has made instant communication possible across large parts of the world. As a result, national controls over information have become less effective. People everywhere are exposed to the

values of other cultures as never before. Yet, although this may enhance mutual understanding across borders, it can also lead to an accentuation of what is distinctive and idiosyncratic in particular cultures, further fragmenting cultural life. Awareness of 'the other' by no means guarantees intersubjective agreement, as the ongoing threats to Salman Rushdie's life after he published *The Satanic Verses* only too clearly showed. Moreover, although the new mass communication industries may generate a distinctive commercial discourse, and a particular set of consumption patterns and values, they confront a multiplicity of languages through which people continue to make sense of their lives and cultures. The available evidence indicates that national and local cultures remain robust. While the 'democratization' of information and communications has changed the nature and form of communication around the world, the diversity of cultures persists, with the most profound consequences.

(6) Globalization has not merely compounded global inequities. While the average incomes in the wealthiest and poorest countries are now further apart than they have ever been – due to the continuing growth of OECD countries while many countries in sub-Saharan Africa and elsewhere have stagnated – the proportion of those who live in the very poorest conditions appears to have declined across the world (see Held and McGrew, 2003, part 3).[2] In addition, the distribution of incomes within some countries has improved. Yet the distributional picture in many places remains complex (CEPR, 2002). For example, while China and India have enjoyed rapid economic growth for two decades and one decade respectively, their rural areas have not grown rapidly and have often suffered prolonged periods of economic stagnation relative to the growth of many urban and coastal areas. This poses serious

---

[2] I say 'appears' because this claim is contested (see chapters 2 and 3). It is difficult to be sure what has happened to global poverty over the recent period since some important data is unreliable. Comparisons with earlier periods are hampered by inadequate samples (especially for China and India), by debatable cost of living indices for the poor, and by the sensitivity of the recorded number of people in poverty to the choice of the benchmark used.

policy challenges at both the national and global levels, but they cannot be reduced to questions about globalization alone.

(7) Globalization has not simply reinforced corporate power. The creation of a global market puts large domestic companies in direct competition with foreign corporations. For example, British Telecom, France Telecom and Deutsche Telekom now have to contend with each other, as they do with a whole range of mobile phone companies like Orange and Vodafone. As one observer aptly noted, 'closed domestic markets, where national champions can cosy up to government, are much more likely to be monopolized than global ones. Even though many global companies are bigger than before, they are not necessarily more powerful. It is the absence of competition, not size, that gives companies clout' (Legrain, 2002, p. 142). Moreover, some of the largest companies depend on the successful sale of brands, and they find that market conditions can quickly change; leading brands such as Levi's, Gap and Xerox have found their market position vulnerable in the face of new and more competitive brands. Furthermore, some of the largest companies investing abroad can create new jobs in, and transfer technology and expertise to, poorer countries. This can be a major bonus to these nations, not a net subtraction from their own power and control. None of this is to say that many large multinational corporations are not very powerful and do not pose major regulatory challenges. Leading MNCs in a number of industries enjoy significant market power and have established international oligopolies. In the developing world, in particular, MNCs are often associated with downward pressures on fiscal and social standards (Vernon, 1998). The mere threat of exit often allows them to elicit concessions from host countries and resist regulation. But it cannot merely be claimed that the multinational corporation today is a monolith able to control its markets and the wider political agenda. The situation is more complicated.

(8) Developing countries as a whole are not losing out in world trade. Over the past decade, developing countries have consistently outperformed developed countries in terms of export growth

– enjoying an average increase of almost 10 per cent a year, compared to 5 per cent for the industrialized countries (Moore, 2003, p. 169). Moreover, trade among developing countries has been growing more rapidly than trade with the industrialized North. Even after 9/11, the export performance of developing countries, measured in terms of trade growth, has been stronger than that recorded by the industrialized economies. Despite an overall decline in trade growth across the world in 2001–2, East Asia and East Europe increased their trade growth. Against this, the Middle East has not increased its share of world trade, and African trade continued to decline. While share of world trade cannot be taken as a general proxy for how well developing countries are doing in the world economy (for, despite increased trade, their share of global GDP has dropped over the last three decades (Doyle, 2000)), some developing countries are clearly doing much better than others. The country-specific and regional disparities in trade growth and economic development need to be understood.

(9) Economic globalization and the current structure of international governance do not exclude the 'voice' and influence of developing countries. For example, development issues are now on the World Trade Organization's agenda. The rule-making and dispute mechanisms of the WTO allow small countries to challenge the power of larger countries. Costa Rica defeated the US under the rule of international law at the WTO. Clearly there are huge asymmetries of power and authority at the global level in relation to both international governmental organizations and the distribution of economic resources. The voting structure of the IMF and World Bank, for example, is heavily weighted in favour of the Group of Seven (G7) (and the Group of One!), with the result that they have a massively disproportionate influence on the governing boards of these intergovernmental organizations (IGOs) and on all aspects of their operations. None the less, politics at the global level cannot be understood simply as the outcome of the preferences of the most powerful. If this were the case, it would not be possible to comprehend the shifting nature of agendas in the leading institutions of global governance.

(10) Popular opposition to dominant political and economic interests is not doomed to fail because it lacks the kinds of resources that most states and multinational companies can command. The growth of international and transnational organizations has altered the form and dynamics of politics. Whereas for most of the last one hundred years international politics was essentially an activity conducted between states, the existence of suprastate organizations, such as the UN and the WTO, has created new arenas in which the voice of peoples can be heard. This voice can be channelled through the web of transnational organizations, groups and movements, often referred to as emerging forces of global civil society (see Anheier, Glasius and Kaldor, 2002). The influence and political impact of these forces can best be measured not in terms of 'hard power' – the capacity to coerce or induce others to change their behaviour – but rather in terms of 'soft power', that is, the capacity to shape others' interests, attitudes, agendas and identities (Nye, 1990). In a media-saturated world, the communicative power of global civil society – the ability to reach a global audience and shape international public opinion – is considerable. Among the more recent and successful campaigns of global civil society are the Jubilee 2000 'drop the debt' campaign, the international coalition for the establishment of the International Criminal Court (ICC), and the Ottawa Convention banning landmines (Held and McGrew, 2002a, ch. 5). While the global order today is shaped by complex constellations of hard and soft power, those that enjoy the former (states and powerful economic interests) by no means always prevail.

The upshot of this critique of popular myths is that globalization is not simply a monolithic, unitary process that brings in its wake wholly positive or negative outcomes. It is formed and constituted by complex processes with multiple impacts which need to be carefully dissected and examined. But one thing is already clear: globalization does not simply lead to the 'end of politics' or the demise of regulatory capacity. Rather, globalization is more accurately linked with the expansion of the terms of political activity, and of the range of actors involved in political life. Globalization marks the continuation of politics by new means operating at many different levels.

Deep drivers and challenges

The challenges posed by the contemporary nature and form of globalization are likely to be of enduring significance. The deep drivers of these processes will be operative for the foreseeable future, irrespective of the exact political form globalization takes. Among these drivers are:

- the changing infrastructure of global communications linked to the IT revolution;
- the development of global markets in goods and services, connected to the new worldwide distribution of information;
- the development of multilayered and multilevel politics, in which nation-states look increasingly 'downward' towards vibrant city and subnational regional politics and 'upward' towards supranational regional and global associations and institutions;
- the end of the Cold War and the diffusion of democratic values across many of the world's regions (alongside some marked reactions to this);
- the internationalization of security in the wake of 9/11 and the proliferation of weapons of mass destruction, and the growing integration of security policies across many countries;
- the deepening of environmental crises and the spread of pandemics such as AIDS/HIV;
- the growth of migration and the movement of peoples, linked to fundamental shifts in demography and the growth of populations;
- the emergence of a new type and form of global civil society, with the crystallization of elements of a global public opinion.

These deeply structured processes can be linked to a number of urgent political and regulatory problems which one writer has referred to as the 'high noon' of our global age (Rischard, 2002). While there are many ways of conceiving and categorizing these issues, Rischard usefully thinks of them as forming three core sets of problems, concerned with sharing our planet, our humanity,

11

Table 1 Twenty global issues

Sharing our Planet: issues involving the global commons
- Global warming
- Biodiversity and ecosystem losses
- Fisheries depletion
- Deforestation
- Water deficits
- Maritime safety and pollution

Sharing our Humanity: issues requiring a global commitment
- Massive step up in the fight against poverty
- Peacekeeping, conflict prevention, combating terrorism
- Education for all
- Global infectious diseases
- Digital divide
- Natural disaster prevention and mitigation

Sharing our Rulebook: issues needing a global regulatory approach
- Reinventing taxation for the twenty-first century
- Biotechnology rules
- Global financial architecture
- Illegal drugs
- Trade, investment and competition rules
- Intellectual property rights
- E-commerce rules
- International labour and migration rules

Source: Rischard, 2002, p. 66

and our rulebook. He lists twenty core challenges under these headings (see table 1). In our increasingly interconnected world, these global problems cannot be solved by any one nation-state acting alone. They call for collective and collaborative action – something that the nations of the world have not been good at, and which they need to be better at if these pressing issues are to be adequately tackled. How we might address the dilemmas and difficulties involved, within a sound social democratic framework, is the subject of the rest of this book.

Introduction

Globalization and social democracy

Before proceeding, a few clarificatory points can usefully be made about globalization and social democracy. In order to begin to understand the challenges posed by globalization to progressive politics and, in particular, to social democracy, it is important to appreciate that the development of social democracy itself depended on two key conditions or institutional compromises – between governors and citizens, on the one side, and between capital, labour and the state, on the other. The first key condition concerns a matter at the heart of liberal democratic thought and practice, involving a posited 'symmetrical' and 'congruent' relationship between political decision-makers and the recipients of political decisions. In fact, symmetry and congruence are assumed at two crucial points: first, between citizen-voters and decision-makers, whom they are, in principle, able to hold to account; and, secondly, between the 'output' (decisions, policies, etc.) of decision-makers and their constituents – ultimately, 'the people' in a delimited territory. It has traditionally been assumed, in other words, by democratic theorists and practitioners, that 'the fate of a national community' is largely in its own hands and that a satisfactory account of democracy can be developed by examining the interplay between actors and processes within the nation-state.

The traditional meaning of social democracy has to be understood in this context. For social democrats sought to deploy the democratic institutions of individual countries on behalf of a particular project: a compromise between the powers of capital, labour and the state which seeks to encourage the development of market institutions, private property and the pursuit of profit within a regulatory framework that guarantees not just the civil and political liberties of citizens, but also the social conditions necessary for people to enjoy their formal rights. Social democrats accepted that markets are central to generating economic well-being, but that in the absence of appropriate regulation they suffer serious flaws, especially the generation of unwanted risks for their citizens and an unequal distribution of those risks, and the creation of negative externalities and inequalities. Assuming the territorial

13

coherence and malleability of national politics, social democrats sought to mould the interests of capital, labour and the state into a balanced package of market economies, social welfare and political regulation. This second condition has been referred to by the concept of 'embedded liberalism' (Ruggie, 1982).

In the post-Second World War period, in particular, many capitalist countries sought to reconcile the efficiency of markets with the values of social community (which markets themselves presuppose) in order to develop and grow. The nature of the balance struck took different forms in different countries, reflecting different national political traditions: in the US, the New Deal, and in Europe, social democracy or the social market economy. Yet the underlying idea was similar: 'a grand social bargain whereby all sectors of society agree to open markets . . . but also to contain and share the social adjustment costs that open markets inevitably produce' (Ruggie, 2003, pp. 93–4). Embedded liberalism built on the accommodation between governors and governed in liberal democracy, and sought to promote both economic liberalization, on the one hand, and social community, on the other. It advocated market-oriented policies alongside the nurturing of social cohesion. This was not simply considered an ethical matter, for the state provision of social goods was regarded as cost effective, while socially cohesive societies avoid the corrosive problems of social conflict. Governments had a key role to play in enacting and managing this programme: moderating the volatility of transaction flows, managing demand levels and providing social investments, safety nets and adjustment assistance.

The contemporary constellation of global forces and networks puts considerable pressure on these conditions. Why? As Ruggie has explained, 'for the industrialized countries, it is the fact that embedded liberalism presupposed an *international* world. It presupposed the existence of *national* economies, engaged in *external* transactions, conducted at *arms length*, which governments could mediate at the *border* by tariff and exchange rates, among other tools' (2003, p. 94). While for a few decades after the Second World War it seemed that a satisfactory balance could be achieved between self-government, social solidarity and international economic openness – at least for the majority of Western countries, and for the majority of their citizens – it now appears that this balance is much harder to sustain. The mobility of capital, goods, people, ideas and pollutants increasingly challenges the capacity of individual governments to sustain their own social and political compromises within delimited borders. New problems are posed by the increasing divergence between the extensive spatial reach of economic and social activity, and the traditional state-based mechanisms of political control. Globalization does not lead to the end of state choice or the end of national political strategies, as noted previously (see pp. 4 and 6), but the regulative capacity of states increasingly has to be matched by the development of collaborative mechanisms of governance at supranational regional and global levels.

The traditional model of social democracy runs into difficulty in this context, for there is increasingly a disjuncture between its proclaimed value orientations and the policy instruments available to realize them. Social democracy has typically been committed to the principles of social justice and social solidarity, on the one hand, and, on the other, to the core principles of liberal democratic politics: the rule of law, political equality and citizenship. The latter were seen as the means to attain the former. Participation in party, electoral and campaigning politics was the vehicle to establish democratic control over the state and to extend it beyond political institutions into social and economic spheres (Lichtheim, 1970; Berki, 1975). The collective organization of society by the state, nationally and locally, became the goal of social democratic politics. To this was frequently added the pursuit of efficiency in public and private life, justified by empirically demonstrable criteria (Barker, 1987). However, in order to achieve efficiency, innovation and entrepreneurship, social democrats came over time to reject a key socialist tenet – the nationalization of the means of production – as a central plank of their programme, and sought to promote market forces within a framework of state-provided public goods and welfare guarantees (see Giddens, 2003). Irrespective of exactly how this programme was implemented in different countries, state-based policy instruments were thought of as the main means for the delivery of social democratic values.

While the values of social democracy – the rule of law, political equality, democratic politics, social justice, social solidarity and economic efficiency – are of enduring significance, the key challenge today is to elaborate their meaning, and to re-examine the conditions of their entrenchment, against the background of the changing global constellation of politics and economics. In the current era, social democracy must be defended and elaborated not just at the level of the nation-state, but at regional and global levels as well. The provision of public goods can no longer be equated with state-provided goods alone. Diverse state and non-state actors shape and contribute to their provision – and they need to do so if some of the most profound challenges of globalization are to be met. Moreover, some core public goods have to be provided regionally and globally if they are to be provided at all. From the establishment of fair trade rules and financial stability to the fight against hunger and environmental degradation, the emphasis is on finding durable modes of international and transnational cooperation and collaboration. With this in mind, the project of global social democracy can be conceived as a basis for promoting the rule of law at the international level; greater transparency, accountability and democracy in global governance; a deeper commitment to social justice in the pursuit of a more equitable distribution of life chances; the protection and reinvention of community at diverse levels; and the regulation of the global economy through the public management of global trade and financial flows, and the engagement of leading stakeholders in corporate governance. These guiding orientations set the politics of global social democracy apart from the pursuit of the Washington consensus, neoliberalism, and the aims of those pitched against globalization in all its forms.

Through the lens of social democratic values, competing policies, political projects and political programmes can be evaluated. A number of social democratic tests can be devised to help demarcate a range of policies and politics for which social democrats can appropriately aim. These tests allow fundamental questions to be asked about choices of policies and politics at all levels, including the global. As a result, competing prescriptions and policy programmes at the global level can be assessed in so far as they:

- promote the rule of law and its impartial application;
- enhance political equality and its core social conditions;
- develop democratic politics through a cluster of rules and institutions permitting the broadest possible participation of citizens in decisions affecting their lives;
- promote social justice by ameliorating the radical asymmetries of life chances that pervade the world today, and by addressing the harm inflicted by these on people against their will and without their consent;
- enhance social solidarity and social integration in so far as they depend on a set of common values and human rights which all human beings can enjoy irrespective of the particular culture or religion within which they are born and brought up;
- pursue economic efficiency and economic effectiveness as far as possible within the constraints of the other tests set out above, and as far as they are compatible with stewardship of the world's environmental resources.

These tests generate a useful filter mechanism for thinking about the nature of contemporary global economic and political processes, and the extent to which their form, dynamic and trajectory are compatible with social democratic ideas, concerns and aspirations. To the extent that they are not, and there are good reasons for being concerned about such a disjuncture, a useful point of orientation is provided to help steer policy choice in a more social democratic direction. It is global social democracy's commitment to all of these values which marks out the contours of its policy agenda. Unlike the positions of its key political opponents – neoconservatism, neoliberalism and radical anti-globalism – its terrain is constituted by the priorities of social justice and solidarity as well as those of the rule of law, democratic politics and effective economic governance. This is the basis of its claim – a claim returned to throughout the volume – to represent a very distinctive form of progressive politics (see Bobbio, 1996).

Part I
ECONOMICS

1

Economic Globalization

The nature and extent of global economic integration is subject to intense dispute (Held and McGrew, 2003, part 4). At issue is whether it is accurate to talk of the emergence of a single borderless global economy; how far such an economy is driven by the new processes of the electronic, information order; and the degree to which the new global economy places constraints on progressive economic and social policy. For some, the new geography of the world economy heralds the emergence of a 'single, planetary scale worldwide economy' (see Dicken, 1998). Led by the growing inter-linking of global and local production systems, the new economic order is increasingly integrated across space, real and virtual. Multi-nationals and global production networks, working on products as diverse as cars, computers and clothes, are reshaping economic activity. The result is a novel form of economic globalization, mediated by the global infrastructures of information and com-munication, functioning as a unit in real or chosen time (Castells, 2000). Regional differences still matter, and many are marginalized and excluded. But, according to the theorists of the global economy, the current world economic order operates with a different form and logic from those found in earlier centuries.

This view is challenged by those who argue that economic globalization is far more limited than is often realized (Hirst and Thompson, 1999; Gilpin, 2001). While they accept that the links between national economies have become more marked, they find that the 'new global economy' is less integrated and inclusive than in the late nineteenth century. Distance and national borders are still 'powerful barriers to economic interaction' (CEPR, 2002). In addition, governments are not as constrained by the open world economy as is often claimed. Macroeconomic policy, along with the social policies underpinning the welfare state, remains the preserve of government. Global markets have not triumphed over states.

The three chapters which follow will not seek to unravel this controversy at length (Held et al., 1999, has sought to do this). Rather, they will seek to depict some of the core trends in the organization of production, trade and finance; the extent to which these are asymmetrical and stratified across countries and regions; and the leading policy and political challenges. The argument is that, irrespective of precisely how one resolves the controversy about economic globalization, clear transformations have occurred in the world economy and they require a new policy mix. The problems of economic globalization are sufficiently urgent to warrant a new political response.

Production, trade and finance

National economies are heavily enmeshed in the global system of production and exchange. Central to this system are rapidly developing multinational corporations (MNCs). Through foreign direct investment or subcontracting arrangements, companies can site almost any value-added activity in any location in the world, subject to adequate infrastructure and human capital reserves. Products that two decades ago were produced in one country are now routinely made up of components that have crossed dozens of borders before they are finally assembled. A new highly specialized geographic division of labour has emerged, recasting the nature and form of production systems. Multinationals span every sector of the global economy – from agriculture to manufacturing and finance – and they have taken economic interconnectedness to new levels. Foreign direct investment (FDI) reached three times as many countries in 2000 as it did in 1985 (UNCTAD, 2001b, p. 4). At present, 60,000 multinational corporations, with nearly 820,000 foreign subsidiaries, sell 15,680 trillion dollars of goods and services across the globe each year, and employ twice as many people as in 1990 (Perraton et al., 1997; UNCTAD, 2001b). Multinational corporations account for about 25 per cent of world production and 70 per cent of world trade, while their sales are equivalent to almost 50 per cent of world GDP (Goldblatt et al., 1997; UNCTAD, 2001b). A quarter to a third of world trade is intrafirm trade between branches of multinationals. While global exports and trading relations are more important than ever in the world economy and to individual countries for their general prosperity, transnational production is even more significant. To sell to another country you have increasingly to invest and have a presence there. To do business with many countries, slicing up the value chain can be a distinct competitive advantage.

The majority of the assets of multinationals are generally found in OECD countries and in a relatively small number of developing ones, but their impact is growing everywhere. Through their production, investment and marketing activities, multinational companies, as a recent Oxfam report put it, 'are linking producers in developing countries ever more closely with consumers in rich countries' (2002, p. 8). From women workers in Bangladesh's garment factories, to workers in China's special economic zones and workers in the free trade zones of Central America, global production networks are generating dense patterns of economic interdependence. Of total world foreign direct investment in 2000, 95 per cent went to 30 countries (UNCTAD, 2001b, p. 5). However, over the last few decades, developing economies' share of foreign investment flows (inward and outward) and of world exports have increased considerably (Castells, 2000; UNCTAD, 1998a, 1998b). The newly industrializing countries of East Asia and Latin America have become an increasingly significant destination for OECD investment and an increasingly important source of OECD imports (Dicken, 1998). By the late 1990s almost 50 per cent of total world manufacturing jobs were located in developing economies, while in 2000 over 65 per cent of developing country exports to the industrialized world were manufactured goods – a thirteenfold increase in less than four decades (UNDP, 1998; World Bank, 2002). For some products, developing country exports account for a half or more of world exports (UNCTAD, 2002b).

The contemporary globalization of production is thus not just an OECD phenomenon, but embraces all regions and continents.

This picture of the transnational organization of production, impressive though it is, does not fully depict the importance of multinational corporations to global economic change. For multinationals form economic relationships with smaller national firms and link them into transnational production chains. They often control the global distribution and transport networks on which independent exporters depend, especially in developing countries, and are of fundamental importance in the creation and transfer of technology across borders. While multinationals typically account for a minority of national production, they are concentrated in the export industries and in the most technologically advanced economic sectors. Hence, as Ulrich Beck put it, 'there is only one thing worse than being dominated by MNCs, and that is not being dominated by MNCs!' (2001).

Linked to the global production system is an extensive network of trading relations. If, in the past, international trade formed an enclave largely isolated from the rest of the national economy, it is now integral to the structure of national production in modern states. All countries are engaged in international trade and nearly all trade significant proportions of their national income. The historical evidence shows that, both in absolute terms and in relation to national income, international trade has grown to unprecedented levels. Measured as a share of GDP, trade levels now are much greater among OECD states than they were in the late nineteenth century (Held et al., 1999, ch. 3). Moreover, as barriers to trade have fallen across the world (in general, tariffs have declined substantially and transportation costs have decreased), global markets have emerged for many goods and, increasingly, services. World trade (trade in merchandise and services) in 1999 was valued at over $6.8 trillion with exports having grown, as a percentage of world output, from 7.9 per cent in 1913 to 17.2 per cent in 1998 (Maddison, 2001).

During the postwar period, an extensive network of international trade emerged which enmeshed most states – developed and developing – in complex webs of global and regional economic relations. Although there are major trading blocs in Europe, North

America and Asia-Pacific, these are not regional fortresses. While they operate complex systems of incentives and disincentives to trade (see chapter 2), these blocs remain open to competition from the rest of the world. As far as economic activity is concerned, regionalization and globalization appear to be mutually reinforcing (Hettne, 1998). This is because regionalism has principally been a vehicle for the liberalization of national economies, a strategy which has taken precedence over the protection of markets (Gamble and Payne, 1991; Hanson, 1998). Through the 1980s and 1990s, developing countries and the transition economies of the former communist bloc have become more open to trade as well. Their share of world trade has risen significantly, particularly in manufactured goods. Across many regions the expansion of trade has been associated with economic growth and rising standards of living. While there is no automatic link between increased trade and reduction of poverty, well-managed integration into global trade networks can lead to higher wages, higher income and a decline in poverty (cf. World Bank, 2001; Oxfam, 2002).

Alongside transnational production and trade networks, the dynamics of finance have become central to economic globalization. World financial flows have grown exponentially, especially since the 1970s. Daily turnover on the foreign exchange markets exceeds $1.2 trillion, and billions of dollars of financial assets are traded globally, particularly through derivative products (BIS, 2001). Few countries are now insulated from the dynamics of global financial markets, although their relationship to these markets differs markedly between North and South (see below). International banking, bond issues and equities trading have risen from negligible levels to historically significant levels measured in relation to world and national output, respectively. The level of cross-border transactions is unprecedented. Where once international financial markets operated to fund wars, trade and long-term investment, a substantial proportion of their activity is now 'speculative'; and this constitutes a significant development. To say that it is speculative, however, is not to say that it is the same as gambling. Many financial institutions and multinational corporations are drawn into the foreign exchange markets in order to hedge against changes in currency valuations and protect their long-term trading position; and financial resources flow across borders, of course, in search of productive investments and future trade opportunities (cf. Strange, 1996). Nonetheless, the annual turnover of foreign exchange markets now stands at an extraordinary figure in excess of sixty-two times the value of world trade. (It was thirteen times world trade in 1979.)

Current levels of cross-border financial flows can induce rapid and volatile movements in the prices of assets, which can increase risks to financial institutions, as the 1998 crisis at the Long Term Capital Management hedge fund and the recent (2001–2) fluctuations in global stock prices (especially in the high-tech sector) both illustrate. In addition, they can reinforce the tendency of financial markets to short-termism, bubbles and overshooting, accentuate the propensity of funds to rapid 'reversibility' faced with uncertainty and risk (especially when trouble in one market leads foreign investors to exit others), and can weaken the prospects of stable, long-term capital flows to the developing world (see Griffith-Jones, 2002; Griffith-Jones and Spratt, 2002). Fluctuations in markets for risk and capital can 'destabilize markets for goods and services, and divert resources from productive activities to unproductive trading in existing assets' (Kay, 2003b, p. 46). As one commentator put it, 'the claims of enormous benefits from free capital mobility are not persuasive. Substantial gains have been asserted, not demonstrated' (Bhagwati, 1998, p. 7).

While free capital markets and the cross-border flows of financial resources do not shape the terms of national economic policy in a straightforward way, they can radically alter the costs of particular policy options and, crucially, policy-makers' perceptions of costs and risks (see Held et al., 1999, ch. 4). Perhaps a key difficulty for policy-makers in these new circumstances is the uncertainty surrounding market responses. There has been a growth of perceived risk in this regard because markets are more liquid than ever before and are an enhanced source of instability. Accordingly, the costs and benefits of pursuing certain policies become fuzzier, and this encourages political caution and 'adaptive policies' – economic and social policies which seek to anticipate market responses.

The 1997–8 East Asian crisis illustrated clearly the changing nature and impact of global financial markets. While the relationship between global financial integration and financial crises is complex, the financial disruption triggered by the collapse of the Thai baht demonstrated new levels of economic interconnectedness (see Bordo et al., 2001; CEPR, 2002, pp. 43–52). The Asian 'tiger' economies had benefited in the 1990s from the rapid increase of financial flows to developing countries and were widely held as models of development for these nations. But the heavy flows of short-term capital were quickly reversed, causing currencies to fall dramatically and far in excess of any real economic imbalances. The effects were disastrous for many East Asian countries. For example, Indonesia's GDP fell in 1998 by 15 per cent, plunging tens of millions of people into poverty and reversing years of successful poverty reduction efforts. In Thailand GDP fell by 8 per cent, causing unemployment to rise and real incomes to decline (Griffith-Jones and Spratt, 2000). The effects of the crisis were experienced worldwide. The inability of the international financial regime (the IMF, Bank for International Settlements (BIS), etc.) to manage the turmoil quickly and effectively created a wide-ranging debate on financial institutional architecture. The latter led to institutional innovations like the Financial Stability Forum and the G20, both convened in 1999 to enhance financial stability and to advance international financial reform. Another important development arose in the 1990s from the recurrent exchange rate crises which became a dominant feature of the global financial system. Between 1990 and 1999 the percentage of countries operating floating exchange rate regimes increased from 21 per cent to 41 per cent (*Financial Times*, 8 Jan. 2002, p. 10). In the context of the growing scale and intensity of global capital flows, the choice that countries faced became increasingly one between (managed) floating rates and monetary union – illustrated by the launch of the euro and discussion of dollarization in parts of Latin America.

It is still too early to be one hundred per cent sure about the full impact of 9/11 on the world economy, but it does seem as if recent global economic trends are broadly unaltered. Since 9/11 the trends towards economic globalization – greater international production, higher trade flows and more integrated product and financial markets – have continued with two important qualifications.[1] The first of these concerns the US. The US has been a major source and recipient of global flows and a major driver of the processes of economic globalization, including greater liberalization and increased market openness. However, 9/11, corporate scandals and the bursting of the dotcom bubble have combined to end the boom of the 1990s and to slow down the development of global economic flows. The second qualification concerns developing and transition countries: global flows to many of these have recently been badly hit by financial crises in Mexico, East Asia, Russia and elsewhere. The integration of developing and transition countries into the world economy is highly volatile and uneven.

Yet global trends in trade have largely continued unabated. The year 2000 recorded the highest levels of trade growth since 1990 and the ratio of world trade to GDP reached 29 per cent. During the 1990s the trade growth of less developed countries more than doubled and stood at more than twice world trade growth. While 2001–2 saw a marked decline in trade growth in the OECD countries and, particularly, in Africa, East Asia and Eastern Europe maintained their trade growth. Overall, the share of developing countries in world trade continued to rise, even though exports from developing economies are still concentrated in a small number of countries and primary goods exporters continue to be marginalized in world economic developments.

After consistently growing faster than trade in recent years, financial flows have been slowing down. Since the 1997 East Asian crisis there has been a decline of financial flows to developing countries; portfolio flows to emerging markets fell after 1997 and, in net terms, banking flows to these countries have been negative. However, the major source of private capital flows to developing and transition economies after 1997 has been FDI. Although there has been continuous growth in FDI flows since 1991, these did fall in 2001 in response to the slowing of US economic activity and 9/11. However, the decline has been more marked in flows to developed countries (down 59 per cent) than to developing

---

[1] I should like to thank Jonathan Perraton for raising these points with me.

countries (down only 14 per cent) and to transition economies (where inflows have actually grown slightly). These figures illustrate the growing global integration of leading LDCs (less developed countries), reflecting the perception of increasing investment opportunities in these countries. It is perhaps surprising that the impact of the US economic slow-down and 9/11 on economic globalization has not been more significant.

It is easy to misrepresent the political significance of the globalization of economic activity. There are those who argue that social and economic processes operate predominantly at the global level, that national political communities are immersed in a sea of global economic flows, and that states are increasingly decision-takers in this context (see, for example, Ohmae, 1990; Gray, 1998). For many neoliberal thinkers, these trends are a welcome development; a world market order based on the principles of free trade and minimum regulation is the guarantee of liberty, efficiency and limited government (see Hayek, 1960, pp. 405–6). By contrast, however, there are those who are more reserved about the extent and benefits of the globalization of economic activity. They point out, for instance, that for all the expansion in global flows of trade and investment, the majority of economic activity still occurs on a more restricted spatial scale – in national economies and in the OECD countries – and that national and international economic management remain feasible (see Hirst and Thompson, 1999; cf. Perraton et al., 1997).

But neither the claims of the global enthusiasts nor those of their critics can be accepted straightforwardly, for both misstate much of what is significant for politics about contemporary economic globalization. Many states in the developed world continue to be immensely powerful, and enjoy access to a formidable range of resources, infrastructural capacities and technologies of regulation and coordination. The continuing lobbying of states and IGOs (for example, the WTO) by MNCs confirms the enduring importance of states and interstate organizations to the mediation and regulation of global economic activity. Yet it would be wrong to argue that economic globalization is a mere illusion, or an ideological veil that allows politicians to disguise the causes of poor performance and policy failure. Among the significant points to stress is the tangible growth in the enmeshment of national economies in global economic transactions – for nearly all countries a growing proportion of national economic activity involves economic exchange with an increasing number of countries. It is this broad increase in the extent, intensity and velocity of economic interconnectedness that has altered the relation between political and economic power. One shift has been especially noteworthy: the historic expansion of exit options in financial markets relative to national capital controls, national banking regulations and national investment strategies, and the sheer volume of privately held capital relative to national reserves. Exit options for corporations making direct investments have also expanded. As a result, the balance of power has, in principle, shifted in favour of capital, *vis-à-vis* both national governments and national labour movements (Goldblatt et al., 1997, p. 281). This does not mean that all business is 'footloose'; rather, it is the fact that businesses can potentially up and move (and a heightened awareness of this by many politicians) that is relevant.

How have government resources and expenditure patterns been affected by these economic transformations? The research and scholarly literature is by no means agreed on the matter. On the one hand, there are those who argue that because of the relative increase in capital mobility and enhanced global market integration, governments are induced to pursue greater fiscal austerity, greater labour market flexibility, a reduction of welfare costs and benefits, and a minimization of regulatory and tax burdens on business. Those who take this position tend to argue that the greater openness of economies is associated with lower rates of capital taxation; that there is a downward pressure on tax rates on all movable factors (on capital, on receipts from investment income and on the highest earners); and that the incidence of tax (where the cost of tax actually falls) tends to be increasingly on labour and other less mobile factors (see Rodrik, 1997; Ganghof, 2000; Hertz, 2001). In addition, a recent comprehensive analysis has found that year-to-year increases in total trade and international financial openness have been associated over the last three decades with less government spending (Garrett, 2000; Garrett and Mitchell, 2001). And another study has shown that in countries where trade union power, centralized collective bargaining and electorally inclusive institutions (proportional representation) are weak, and where public authority is dispersed or fragmented, international capital mobility is linked with pressure to reduce the public economy, social transfers and public consumption (see Swank, 2001).

While the extent of these changes remains small, with patterns varying among countries (and foreign direct investment is not associated with such negative effects), these tendencies have led some to argue that they signal 'a gradual shift in the political economy of industrialized countries, away from an earlier "compensatory" approach to managing the effects of increased openness, towards more of a "competitiveness" model' (Ruggie, 2003, p. 99). In short, embedded liberalism and social democracy have gradually given way to a set of economic and social policies focused on market adaptation and flexibility (see Swank, 2002b).

Against these claims, there are those who take a much more cautious view of the research findings to date. They suggest that there is no firm evidence that economic globalization has led to a decline in taxes on company earnings, or in labour and welfare standards. They find no good reason for thinking that government regulatory capacity is diminishing in relation to corporations and markets. Those in this camp recognize that 'some corporations do indeed evade government taxation and regulatory control, and extreme vigilance is certainly required' (CEPR, 2002, p. 104). But they argue that there is no overall evidence that government regulation of business is weakening. In addition, these analysts recognize that while it is true that the share of business taxes has fallen in a number of countries, 'there is only weak evidence that greater mobility of capital has resulted in systematic changes in the tax structure, and no evidence at all that it has resulted in a fall in overall revenues compared to earlier periods. If anything, the continuing upward drift in the share of taxes in GDP suggests a strong underlying tendency for government to grow' (CEPR, 2002, p. 7; see also Garrett and Mitchell, 2001). The evidence in table 2 is relevant in this regard. This table compares, for a range of OECD countries, both overall tax burdens between 1970 and 1998, and the shares of profits and other taxes in the overall tax revenue

Table 2 Tax levels and composition for various OECD countries, 1970, 1980 and 1997–1998

	Tax burden (% GDP)			of which: Profit taxes		Employment taxes		Sales/ VAT	
	1970	1980	1998	1980	1997	1980	1997	1980	1997
Canada	31.3	30.3	43.4	11.6	10.3	44.6	51.4	32.6	24.4
France	37.4	43.6	50.9	5.1	5.8	55.6	54.6	30.4	27.8
Germany	37.2	43.9	44.8	5.5	4.0	64.2	65.5	27.1	27.7
Italy	27.9	32.4	46.4	7.8	9.5	61.1	58.8	26.5	25.9
Japan	19.7	25.6	30.8	21.8	15.0	53.4	57.4	16.3	16.5
UK	35.6	35.3	40.6	8.3	12.1	46.6	42.0	29.2	35.0
USA	28.9	30.0	34.4	10.8	9.4	65.3	63.2	16.6	16.7

Employment taxes include individual income taxes and social security contributions.
Source: CEPR, 2002, p. 84; derived from *Statistical Abstract of the United States: Comparative International Statistics*, various years

between 1980 and 1997. Although the 1980s were widely regarded as a tax-cutting period, the table discloses that

> in the main in industrialized countries the tax burden continued to rise steadily, as it had in the 1970s . . . . The share of business taxes in that burden fell in some countries, while taxes on employment rose in Canada, Germany and Japan. Overall there is only weak evidence that greater mobility of capital has resulted in systematic changes in the tax structure, and none that it has resulted in a fall in overall revenues. (CEPR, 2002, p. 85)

Accordingly, in this second, more sceptical view, global economic integration does not hinder the capacity of governments to regulate their economies and adjust their own policies to their particular economic conditions; moreover, it probably enhances this capacity in the long run because of benefits that derive overall from better economic performance. Again, it is stressed, the evidence is not yet strong in many areas and many of the measured effects must be regarded as tentative. But the main conclusion is that economic difficulties and domestic problems are often due to insufficient globalization rather than too much of it.

The debate about economic globalization and its policy impact needs to be broken down further if more analytical progress on these issues is to be made; for economic globalization embraces a diverse set of processes with uneven effects across the world's regions and countries. There are marked asymmetries of impact. These asymmetries often result in very little room to shape and manoeuvre policy in the poorest countries. This important finding arises from looking at patterns of globalization, stratification and inequality.

2

Globalization,
Stratification and Inequality

The gulf between the richest and poorest in the global order can be mapped in the form of a champagne glass (see figure 1 opposite). This stark portrayal of the global distribution of income dramatically illustrates the huge disparities in the economic resources made available to the world's population. These disparities can be illuminated further by noting that the 900 million people lucky enough to reside in the Western world enjoy 86 per cent of world consumption expenditures, 79 per cent of world income, 58 per cent of world energy consumption and 74 per cent of all telephone lines. By comparison, the poorest 1.2 billion of the world's population have to share only 1.3 per cent of world consumption, 4 per cent of world energy consumption, 5 per cent of world fish and meat consumption and 1.5 per cent of all telephone lines.

For many commentators on globalization, global inequality is the most critical issue on the contemporary global agenda. Yet the debate about its causes and consequences is complex. The principal division is between those who understand global inequality as the inevitable product of two centuries of industrialization in the West and who interpret globalization as a powerful force for spreading wealth and reducing poverty, and those who argue that it is doing the opposite; that is, creating a more impoverished and unequal world. Table 3 sets out some of the core historical trends. While the data on global inequality and poverty is incomplete and patchy for many parts of the world (notably, India, China and large parts of Africa), it is not unreasonable to claim that five developments are occurring simultaneously:

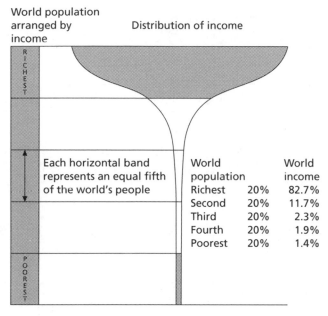

Figure 1 The 'champagne glass' pattern of inequality between the world's rich and poor
Source: Wade, 2001

1   The absolute gap between the world's richest and poorest states is now the largest it has been, and it is getting larger: although the number of people living in extreme poverty (defined as subsisting on less than $1 per day) has remained constant in recent times, the number living on $2 per day has increased (see Held and McGrew, 2003, part 5).

2   The proportion of the world's population living in extreme poverty appears to be falling; it has declined compared to twenty years ago, and may be at its lowest level ever (World Bank, 2002; Wade, 2003; cf. Reddy and Pogge, 2003). Moreover, for nearly all countries, the human development index – which assesses a country's progress in terms of longevity (measured by life expectancy at birth), knowledge (measured by a combination of the adult literacy rate and the combined gross primary, secondary and tertiary enrolment ratio), and standard of living (measured by GDP per

Table 3 World distribution of income and life expectancy: inequality and poverty indices for selected years

	1820	1870	1910	1929	1950	1970	1992
Mean world income (PPP $ 1990)	658.7	890.0	1459.9	1817.1	2145.5	3773.8	4962.0
World population (millions)	1057.0	1266.0	1719.0	2042.1	2511.3	3664.5	5459.1
Income shares							
Top 10%	42.8	47.6	50.9	49.8	51.3	50.8	53.4
Bottom 20%	4.7	3.8	3.0	2.9	2.4	2.2	2.2
Share of top 10% divided by bottom 20%	9.1	12.4	16.8	17.2	21.2	23.4	23.8
Summary inequality measures							
Coefficient of Gini	0.500	0.560	0.610	0.616	0.640	0.650	0.657
Standard deviation of logarithm	0.826	0.919	1.027	1.064	1.154	1.210	1.184
Poverty headcount (%)							
Poverty ($2 per day, inflation-adjusted)	94.4	89.6	8.24	75.9	71.9	60.1	51.3
Extreme poverty ($1 per day)	83.9	75.4	65.6	56.3	54.8	35.6	23.7
Poverty headcount (millions)							
Poverty ($2 per day)	997.8	1134.3	1416.5	1550.5	1805.6	2200.7	2800.5
Extreme poverty ($1 per day)	886.8	954.0	1127.7	1149.7	1376.2	1304.7	1293.8
Life expectancy							
Mean	26.5	32.8	32.8	38.5	50.1	59.4	61.1
Theil index (between countries)	0.012	0.045	0.045	0.046	0.025	0.012	0.013

Source: CEPR, 2002, table 8, p. 57; originally from Bourguignon and Morrisson, 2002, table 1

capita (PPP US $)) – has gone up in recent years. Between 1995 and 2000 there were just eleven countries for which the index went down, nine of them from Africa (Kenya, Zimbabwe, Botswana, Swaziland, Namibia, South Africa, Malawi, Lesotho and Burundi), and the remaining two being Moldova and Tajikistan (UNDP, 2002).[1]

3   There are rapidly diverging patterns of life chances between men and women. Severe forms of impoverishment, social exclusion and inequality are particularly virulent among women. Today, poverty and ill-health all too often have 'a woman's face' (as Kofi Annan recently put it). Seventy per cent of the 1.2 billion people living on less than a dollar a day are women; the increase in the number of people in poverty in rural areas is 17 per cent higher for women than for men over a two-decade period; and twice as many women as men are among the world's 900 million illiterates (Rouleau, 2002; cf. Steans, 2002).

4   There are significant shifts in between-region and between-country patterns of economic inequality; that is to say, countries and regions can move up or down the world's stratification hierarchy.

5   Within-country inequality has increased since the 1980s in several countries, for example in Asia (China, Thailand, Malaysia) and Latin America (Chile, Colombia, Mexico), while improving or remaining stable in others (CEPR, 2002, ch. 4.3).

These points highlight that while economic development and globalization may well be working for many people in a significant range of countries, they are by no means yet working for all. A more careful look at the stratification of trade, finance and production networks illuminates this point further.

---

[1]   The falls in the human development index among African countries are due, in part, to the effects of the AIDS pandemic. It can also be noted that although the human development index may not have fallen for most of the ex-Soviet republics over 1995 to 2000, in none of these countries had the index reached its 1990 level by 2000. In this regard, most of the ex-Soviet republics are still struggling.

The stratification of economic activity

Developed states have dominated postwar trade in goods.[2] In 1950 they accounted for 64 per cent of world exports, in 1970 for 75 per cent and in 1996 70 per cent. From the 1950s until the early 1980s any decline or fluctuation in their share of world trade was closely mirrored by changes in the share attributable to oil-exporting countries. In 1980 developed countries' share of both world exports and imports of goods was 63.82 per cent, while it was 28.64 per cent for developing countries. In 1990 the share for developed countries rose to 71.43 per cent; for developing countries it sank back to 23.93 per cent. By 1995 this tendency was, however, reversed and shares were 68.59 per cent and 27.81 per cent, respectively. This trend continued to 2000, when the shares were 63.89 per cent and 32.12 per cent (UNCTAD, 2001b). It is also reflected in the 2001 data (see figure 2). It is only since the mid-1980s that oil-importing developing countries as a whole have expanded their share of world trade relative to both oil exporters and the developed economies. Moreover, much of this growth in trade share is attributable to the rise of the East Asian economies. Although these figures are for merchandise trade, the patterns are similar for trade in services.

Trade has played a key role in the performance of individual developing countries, leading to differential performances among them. Accordingly, in economic terms, these countries can no longer be seen as a homogeneous bloc facing common external conditions. Many East Asian countries have achieved rapid economic growth and are now among the richest industrializing economies. The pattern of exports for these countries is significantly different from that of other developing countries. They have enjoyed relatively high levels of investment, both domestic and foreign, and have expanded their capacity to trade. Although growth in these countries has not just been export generated, exporting to world markets has been central to maintaining the profitability of their investments and thus sustaining growth rates, especially after the 1997–8 crisis.

[2] This section is adapted and updated from material first presented in Held et al., 1999, chs 3–5.

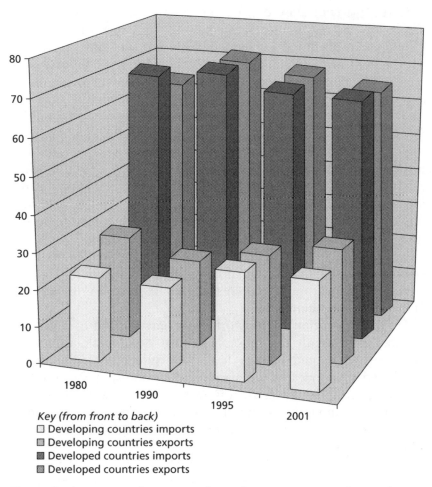

Figure 2 Imports and exports of goods as percentage share of world total
Source: UNCTAD, 2002a, pp. 14–15

A significant group of newly industrializing economies – particularly those concentrated in East Asia – grew rapidly throughout the 1980s and mid-1990s, exporting manufactured goods to OECD economies. As the most successful of these moved out of low wage production, other poorer economies filled their places. Some of the latter have since prospered in the world economy. For others, industrial growth slowed with exposure to global competition. Those low income countries, particularly in Africa, that failed to develop manufactured or service-based exports have remained exporters of primary commodities. Although trade conditions for primary products have varied throughout the postwar era, these exporters have tended to face, at best, sluggish markets. In the early 1980s, for example, demand for most primary commodities fell sharply, and with it prices. These falls had a huge negative impact on primary exporters and in many cases growth rates and investment levels have still not recovered. Fifty of the world's poorest countries, in fact, depend for over half their export earnings on three or fewer primary commodities. Today, low and unstable prices for such commodities are a major factor hindering trade from working for many of them (see Oxfam, 2002). For example, since 1997 coffee prices have fallen by over 70 per cent, costing developing country exporters some $8 billion in lost foreign exchange earnings, and creating severe hardship for already vulnerable communities.

Trade competition in the world economy has led to diverging income levels, with the most successful developing economies achieving per capita income levels equivalent to some poorer developed economies, while many of the poorest states confront declining terms of trade. In this respect, the new international division of labour emerging in the world economy embodies new patterns of 'winners' and 'losers', creating diverging forms of stratification.

Alongside changes in the structure of world trade, there have been marked transformations in the extent and intensity of the global financial system, with important distributional implications. While the poorest developing countries remain largely excluded from private financial markets and are dependent on official aid and loans (plus small amounts of FDI) to support investment, for the first time since the interwar period many developing countries and East European transition economies are now reincorporated as borrowers into international capital markets. The cost of incorporation varies. Whereas OECD countries may on occasion have to pay a premium on the cost of borrowing, countries considered to be higher risk by the international credit rating agencies, such as

Moody's or Standard and Poor, will have more costly or limited access to private international finance.

Until the 1990s access to international finance for developing countries and emerging economies was limited to aid, FDI, IGO loans and bank loans, with access to international bank loans largely confined to a small number of East Asian economies. Moreover, for much of the postwar era, developing countries have had minimal access to international bond markets. Very few companies from developing countries issued shares internationally, and few institutional investors in the developed world acquired shares from developing country markets as part of their portfolios. All these key forms of private international finance were almost completely confined to the OECD states until the early 1990s. Since then, domestic financial markets in developing countries have been opened up to international investors and these countries, alongside transition economies, have received significant financial inflows. Most notably, Latin America regained access to private international capital markets: net outflows over 1983–9 of $116 billion switched to net inflows of $200 billion over 1990–4. In 2001, Latin America was the largest regional recipient of private capital inflows, despite a substantial decline in flows to Argentina in the light of its mounting economic difficulties. Other regions, with the exception of the Middle Eastern countries and Turkey, also received positive inflows. According to estimates from the Institute of International Finance, Latin America received $58.3 billion in capital inflows in 2000, $47.8 billion in 2001 and $51.1 billion in 2002 (UNCTAD, 2002b). However, according to the UN Economic Commission for Latin America and the Caribbean (ECLAC), there were outflows in 2002 of $39 billion, half of those explained by the crisis in Argentina (ECLAC, at www.eclac.org).

In addition, it is interesting to note that some developing countries have recently issued international bonds in significant quantities for the first time in the postwar period, and some companies in these countries have issued international equities for the first time ever. International investors were attracted to some emerging markets by relatively high interest rates, particularly in Latin America. They were also attracted by the prospect of expanding

41

markets and aimed to diversify their holdings as they took an increasingly global view of their portfolios.

Of the world's developing regions, East Asia and Latin America have tended to dominate private capital flows, although the transition economies of the former communist bloc have attracted an increasing share. By the late 1990s private capital flows to developing countries were higher in relation to either their GDP or investment levels than during the 1970s. However, these flows declined sharply following the East Asian currency crises of 1997–8.[3] FDI flows to the poorest economies, notably those in Africa, remain less than 1 per cent of the total. Nonetheless, it is worth noting that the ratio of official development aid to gross fixed investment in these countries is around two-thirds; thus, although these countries have very limited access to international finance, their economic development is still linked in important respects to private international financial resources. By comparison, the transition economies have attracted a growing share of financial flows.

Developing countries and the transition economies are, accordingly, incorporated into the global financial system, but in a manner that is strongly uneven and hierarchical. Some developing countries have had access to private international borrowing, but have also periodically faced credit rationing. In the 1990s increased capital flows linked their emerging stock markets more closely with world markets. But the poorest countries have remained on the margins of private international finance. Indeed, in the late 1990s as many as ninety countries were under various forms of IMF adjustment programmes.

Patterns of multinational production and FDI across the world also reveal distinct and highly uneven forms. Throughout the postwar period MNCs from just eight countries – the G5 economies plus the Netherlands, Sweden and Switzerland – accounted for

---

[3] Shifts in capital flows illustrate the more general point (see pp. 26–7) about the volatility of these flows, and their problematic role as a durable basis for development finance. While most developing countries were largely cut off from private finance in the 1980s, there were sharp inflows in the early 1990s, which caused adjustment problems, followed by a reversal after the 1997–8 crisis. Much of the Latin American total of private capital flows over the past five years appears to be FDI with little net portfolio flow and negative bank flows (see Griffith-Jones, 2002; Griffith-Jones and Spratt, 2002; Eatwell and Taylor, 2000).

over two-thirds of world FDI stocks, although there have been some important distributional shifts. The US has been the largest overseas investor and its FDI stock has continued to grow, but its share of global FDI has fallen, from around 50 per cent in 1960 to less than 25 per cent today. Similarly, the shares of Britain and the Netherlands, two major traditional investors, have fallen over this period even though their FDI stocks have also risen in absolute terms. Conversely, German and Japanese firms have sharply increased their share of world FDI stocks from negligible levels in the 1960s to substantial shares, with German firms now having the third largest holdings of FDI, and Japanese the fifth. FDI from developing countries, which has also grown steadily, reached record levels (after a decrease in 1998) in 2000 (UNCTAD, 2001a). Moreover, whereas in the 1950s and 1960s almost all of the world's largest firms were based in OECD states, a small but growing number of MNCs based in developing countries have also achieved global prominence (Bergesen and Fernandez, 1995; Dicken, 1998; CEPR, 2002). Nevertheless, the vast majority of MNCs and FDI flows originate within, and move among, OECD countries.

Yet, having recorded this continuing OECD economic dominance, it is worth emphasizing that the concentration of FDI flows (as opposed to stocks) among OECD states has been falling: 'there has been a steady decline in their share of global [FDI] inflows since 1989' (UNCTAD, 1997, p. 3). FDI outflows from developing countries are growing as well, as noted, although they account for less than 10 per cent of global FDI stocks.[4] Recent evidence suggests that these FDI trends are continuing (UNCTAD, 2001a). This picture is reinforced by the geography of cross-border mergers and acquisitions. Such activity is becoming less concentrated among OECD states and more widely diffused. These are important developments which distinguish the present era from earlier historical phases of cross-border economic activity.

The extent of FDI is such that virtually all countries in the world have some FDI stocks, although the levels vary widely.

---

[4] The distinction between FDI stocks and flows is significant since the former measures historically accumulated FDI, while the latter measures inflows or outflows of FDI over time.

Since the early 1970s, the share of FDI of the top ten developing countries has risen from less than half to around two-thirds of FDI stocks in developing countries (calculated from UNCTC, 1983 and UNCTAD, 1996). Africa has become more marginalized with the decline of FDI in primary production. Latin America remains an important location, despite significant shifts in its share of inward FDI over the last twenty-five years. The most dramatic rise has been, again, in East Asia, although this trend suffered a setback in the aftermath of the regional economic crisis. China, in particular, has received large inflows of FDI because MNCs perceive vast growth potential as it undergoes economic transformation. In 2002, China became the world's largest recipient of FDI, drawing in $53 billion (although its current status as the single largest focus of FDI has, despite very significant FDI growth, more to do with the collapse in 2002 of FDI to the US (Economist, 2003)).

As noted previously, there are also significant (and increasing) levels of FDI outflows from developing countries and a significant number of parent MNCs based in these economies. Between 1993 and 1995 the foreign assets of the fifty largest MNCs based in developing countries increased by some 280 per cent compared to a 30 per cent increase for the world's top hundred (almost exclusively OECD) MNCs (UNCTAD, 1997, p. 8). Patterns of global production are, as a result, becoming more complex in respect of ownership and control.

These shifting patterns of stratification of international production reflect not only a more complex global division of labour but also changing sectoral patterns of global production. Immediately after the Second World War the majority of FDI was concentrated in the primary product sector. But FDI in primary products has declined. This is not only because of the general decline of primary production in the world economy, but because many developing countries nationalized raw material production during the Cold War. MNCs in these industries typically responded by concentrating on the refining and distribution of raw materials, although a number of large MNCs continue to dominate extractive or agricultural operations as well.

MNCs today account for the majority of the world's manufacturing exports. Given increased international sourcing from both affiliates and subcontractors, trade in intermediate products (unfinished goods) has risen as MNCs stretch the production process transnationally. MNCs are thereby creating a new global division of labour as production is organized worldwide to take advantage of lower production costs or particular national conditions. Although a significant proportion of FDI is concentrated in manufacturing, FDI in services has also expanded enormously and now accounts for a growing proportion of international business activity and of FDI stocks. Most of this activity remains concentrated in the traditional areas of banking and trade, but it has grown recently in other sectors, including financial and business services, data processing and tourism.

Political strategies and the pattern of winners and losers

The absolute gulf between the richest and the poorest states, whether measured in terms of income, health or education, has been accelerating (Bradshaw and Wallace, 1996). In 1960, the income of the richest 20 per cent of the world's people stood at about thirty times that of the poorest 20 per cent; by 1997 the corresponding multiple was seventy-four (UNDP, 1997). Today, the richest 5 per cent of the world's people have incomes 114 times those of the poorest 5 per cent; and the richest 1 per cent receive as much income each year as the poorest 57 per cent (UNDP, 2002). The absolute gap is getting wider faster, and this matters because it reinforces patterns of inclusion and exclusion in the world economy, and makes the gulf between the empowered and the disempowered harder to bridge.

However, there are vast differences between regions, with East and South Asia rapidly closing the income gap, while for sub-Saharan Africa the gap is still widening (UNDP, 2001). Between 1975 and 2000, per capita income (PPP) in East Asia and the Pacific increased from about a fourteenth of the average income in OECD countries to more than a sixth. In sub-Saharan Africa the trend was reversed, dropping from a sixth to a fourteenth – the worst case representing less than one-fortieth. In Latin America

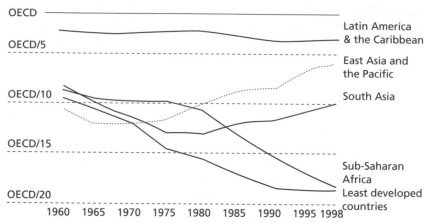

OECD

OECD/5 — Latin America & the Caribbean

East Asia and the Pacific

OECD/10 — South Asia

OECD/15

OECD/20 — Sub-Saharan Africa / Least developed countries

1960 1965 1970 1975 1980 1985 1990 1995 1998

High income OECD excludes OECD members classified as developing countries and those in Eastern Europe and the former Soviet Union.

Figure 3 Comparing incomes between the developing regions and high income OECD, 1960–1998 (regional average GDP per capita (1985 US$ PPP) as a ratio of that of high income OECD countries)
Source: UNDP, 2001, p. 16, based on World Bank data

there was a slight deterioration, with incomes decreasing from a little less than one-half to a little less than a third of the OECD average (UNDP, 2002). During the 1990s extreme poverty (subsistence levels of less than a dollar a day) halved in East Asia and the Pacific and fell by 7 per cent in South Asia, while the proportion of people in extreme poverty in sub-Saharan Africa fell only very marginally, and the number of people in such poverty rose from 242 million to 300 million. Twenty sub-Saharan countries (with more than half the region's population) are poorer now than in 1990, and twenty-four are poorer than in 1975.

While there is general acceptance that the global structure of economic power shapes the context, and constrains the nature, of economic development, the fact that many states in East Asia and Latin America grew rapidly throughout the 1980s and 1990s highlights the vital role played by effective economic governance and national development strategies. Indeed, the growing divergence in the economic fortunes of developing states, highlighted in figure 3, suggests that patterns of global inequality and poverty are not dictated solely by the historical dominance of the Western economies. In short, as stated in the Introduction, states still matter. In addition, national or local factors, such as resource endowments, are of clear significance in helping to lift nations and communities out of poverty (Gilpin, 2001; Hirst, 1997; Weiss, 1998; Moore, 2003). Globalization must not blind observers to the ways in which states can continue to use their power 'to implement policies to channel economic forces in ways favourable to their own national interests and . . . a favourable share of the gains from international economic activities' (Gilpin, 2001, p. 21). Concomitantly, increased global inequality and poverty can be understood, at least in part, as the product of state failures.

Having noted this, it should not be concluded that developmental strategies designed to address, and ameliorate the worst consequences of, global inequality can be focused solely on building local and national state capacity, important though this is. Many of the poorest countries, especially those most heavily indebted and with minimum or no physical infrastructure, cannot easily find a successful entry point into the highly competitive world economic and political order. In fact, according to some commentators, they have just about dropped out of the world trading system and are in danger of dropping out of the world economic order altogether (see, for example, Moore, 2003).

While the distributive consequences of globalization are highly debated, research, initially published on the web by Geoffrey Garrett, suggests that globalization is by no means equally good for all countries at different phases of development (2001). Or, to put the point more fully, integration into trade and financial markets has different consequences for countries at different stages of development. After examining the distributive effects of globalization (conceived in the study as international market integration measured in terms of trade, FDI and openness to global capital movements) for countries divided into three categories – high, medium and low income[5] – Garrett concluded that there is a

---

[5] This division follows the World Bank categorization (2000). The high income group comprises fifty countries with per capita national incomes above $9,360 (in constant 1985 dollars, PPP); the middle income group comprises ninety-three countries with per capita incomes between $760 and $9,360; low income countries have per capita incomes below $760.

minimum development threshold for benefiting from globalization, in terms of human capital, physical infrastructure and political institutions, and that low income countries have by and large not yet reached this threshold (2001, p. 4).

How might global market integration hinder or retard the development of the world's poorest countries? The standard explanation is that low income countries are in a development trap; that is to say, poor socioeconomic conditions (the fact that many such countries are landlocked, tropical, highly dependent on natural resources, ethnically heterogeneous, and have low life expectancy and high fertility rates) combine with bad political conditions (typically, authoritarian regimes, weak and/or corrupt governmental institutions, inadequate investment in education and learning) to check and undermine the convergence logic of economic theory. The latter suggests that globalization should help poor countries to benefit from the comparative advantage they enjoy, and to diversify their economic activity. There are some conditions of geography and climate that, of course, policy-makers can make little difference to. But there are others that political actors can improve. While it is hard to isolate precisely which factors have been uppermost in accounting for the negative impact of globalization on low income countries, poor human capital (educational attainment, life expectancy and fertility), corrupt and/or autocratic governance and weak market institutions have played a contributing role in some countries being 'overwhelmed' by globalization. The consequences include the exacerbation of poverty and inequality, the erosion of traditional ways of life, and the exposure of nations to unstable and volatile market conditions.

There appears to be a minimum level of economic and political development below which the benefits of international market integration are not realized, and indeed, below which the effects can be extremely detrimental. While it is hard to draw an exact economic line to demarcate those countries that will benefit from those that will not, the conventional low versus middle income categorization used by the World Bank seems a reasonable approximation. If this analysis is sound, the implications of the argument are also clear. Global economic integration alone cannot be adequate medicine for low income countries to escape a development trap. While it would be wrong to argue in favour of widespread protectionism, sequencing openness in a set of reforms, and only advocating openness once substantial progress has been made in relation to the development of human capital, physical infrastructure and independent political institutions, is a sensible way to proceed (Garrett, 2001). This position sets down a direction in policy which is, in fact, similar to that taken by the World Bank itself in the last few years. Globalization *per se* is neither good nor bad; it works best under complex sets of social, economic, cultural and political conditions, all or many of which need to be present if the world's poorest countries are to be robust enough to engage productively in the contemporary economic processes of globalization. Globalization can and does create complex patterns of winners and losers, and it is important to attempt to adjust development policy to improve the position of the least well-off while not eroding the processes of globalization that have been beneficial for, broadly speaking, higher income countries over the last two decades or so.

Since Garrett placed his paper on the web, he has recast his study and modified his findings in important respects (forthcoming). He now argues that the key global factor impacting on the capacity of the poorest countries to develop is not tariff liberalization, but capital liberalization. Tariff liberalization, linked to sound strategies for economic and political development, has been beneficial for low income countries. By contrast, rapid capital liberalization, as indicated in chapter 1, can be a recipe, in the absence of prudential regulation and sound domestic capital markets, 'for volatility, unpredictability and booms and busts in capital flows'. Countries that have rapidly opened their capital accounts (for example, Zambia) have performed significantly less well (in terms of economic growth and income inequality) than countries that have maintained tight control on capital movements and cut tariffs. Interestingly, Garrett's new study shows that middle income countries, which have experienced a rapid reduction of restrictions on both trade and capital, can also be economically vulnerable, squeezed between the products of low income countries and the high technology output of richer countries.

The experience of China and India – along with Japan, South Korea and Taiwan in earlier times – shows that countries do not

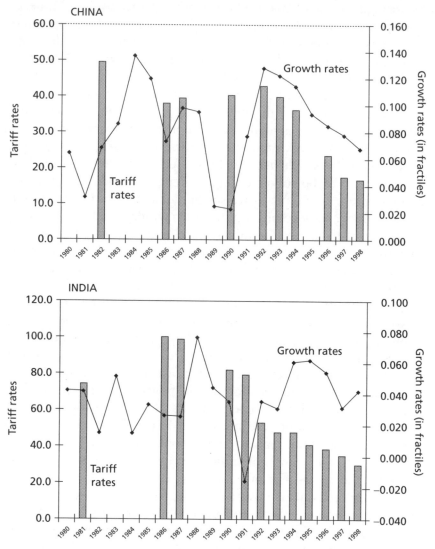

Figure 4 China's and India's real annual GDP per capita growth rate, and average weighted tariffs, 1980–1998
Source: Milanovic, 2003, p. 677: growth rates from World Bank SIMA database; tariff rates from Francis Ng (World Bank)

have to adopt, first and foremost, liberal trade and/or capital policies in order to benefit from enhanced trade, to grow faster, and to develop an industrial infrastructure able to produce an increasing proportion of national consumption. All these countries, as Robert Wade has recently argued, have experienced relatively fast growth behind protective barriers, growth which fuelled rapid trade expansion focused on capital and intermediate goods (2003, pp. 31–3). As each of these countries has become richer, it has tended to liberalize its trade policy. Accordingly, it is a misunderstanding to say that trade liberalization *per se* has fuelled these countries' economic growth; rather, it is the case that these countries developed relatively quickly behind protective barriers, before they liberalized their trade: see figure 4. If it is the case that these countries, and others like them, did not straightforwardly develop as a result of trade liberalization, and if it is the case that some of the poorest countries of the world are worse off as a result of an excessive haste with respect to global capital market integration, then the case is strengthened for applying the precautionary principle to global economic integration and revisiting development prescriptions. While economic protectionism is to be resisted as a general strategy, there is much evidence to suggest that a country's *internal* economic integration – the development of its human capital, its economic infrastructure and robust national market institutions, and the replacement of imports with national production where feasible – needs to be stimulated by state-led economic and industrial policy. The evidence suggests that higher internal economic integration can help generate the conditions from which a country can benefit from higher *external* integration.[6] This finding should not come as a surprise since nearly all of today's developed countries initiated their growth behind tariff barriers, and only lowered these once their economies

---

[6] It is useful to clarify the distinction between internal and external integration. Integration in today's development discourse, as Wade explains, 'refers to integration of a national economy into world markets, or external integration, and it is [erroneously] taken for granted that more external integration will automatically stimulate more internal integration between sectors (rural–urban, consumer goods–intermediate goods, etc.) and between wages, consumption, and production' (2003, p. 42).

were relatively robust. They did not begin their development by rapidly opening their economies to foreign trade, capital flows and investment.

While integration into global trade and financial markets can offer poorer countries significant benefits, especially when they are part of a coherent poverty reduction strategy, without such a strategy it can be more damaging than constructive. Strong arguments for rapid trade and financial liberalization have been made by the IMF, the World Bank, and many governments in the North over the last twenty to thirty years. In the case of the IMF and the World Bank, their advocacy of these arguments has been backed by strong loan conditionality which required developing countries to reduce their economic barriers. But the result of this has often been, as a recent Oxfam report points out, that 'poor countries have been opening up their economies much more rapidly than rich countries. Average import tariffs have been halved in sub-Saharan Africa and South Asia, and cut by two-thirds in Latin America and East Asia' (2002, p. 12).[7] Oxfam has mounted a persuasive challenge to the IMF and World Bank position which traditionally asserted that trade and capital liberalization is good for growth, and that the poor share in the benefits of growth on an equitable basis. The evidence and studies drawn on here also challenge this finding, with important policy implications. The upshot of these is that improved global market access is only one of the core requirements for enhancing the links between trade, finance, growth and poverty reduction. Many of the poorest countries lack the means and infrastructure to take advantage of new market openings. To fully benefit from the process of economic globalization, they require the development of a series of economic, social, cultural and economic conditions which, together, combine to help make market access productive in the short and

[7]   It can be argued that poor countries need to reduce tariff barriers particularly rapidly since developing countries have generally higher trade barriers than developed countries (Bhagwati, 2002). While there is some truth to this, the argument developed here is that in order to benefit from such reductions, the poorest countries need a diverse range of domestic and international reforms to be in place (see below).

long term. For prosperity and economic development, globalization alone is not enough: a complex array of policy packages is necessary at diverse levels – national, supraregional and global.

There is no single route to economic development; knowledge of local conditions, experimentation with suitable domestic institutions and the nurturing of internal economic integration need to be combined with sound macroeconomic policy and some aspects of external market integration. The most successful recent cases of development – East Asia, China, India – have managed to find ways of taking advantage of the opportunities offered by world markets – cheaper products, exports, technology and capital – while entrenching domestic incentives for investment and institution building. As Dani Rodrik has succinctly put it:

> Market incentives, macroeconomic stability, and sound institutions are key to economic development. But these requirements can be generated in a number of different ways – by making the best use of existing capabilities in light of resources and other constraints. There is no single model of a successful transition to a high growth path. Each country has to figure out its own investment strategy. (2001, p. 22)

While asymmetries of global market access (including selective protectionism, tariff barriers in the developed and developing world, European and American subsidies in agriculture and textiles and so on) are a pressing problem, an exclusive focus on this can distort development strategies. Development thinking has to shift from a dogged focus on 'market access' to a more complex mindset (see Rodrik, 2001). Developing nations need policy space to exercise institutional innovations that depart from the prevailing orthodoxies of the World Bank, IMF and WTO. Concomitantly, organizations like the WTO need to move their agenda away from a narrow set of policies concerned with market creation and supervision to a broader range of policies which encourage different national economic systems to flourish within a fair and equitable rule-based global market order.

The other side of this position is, of course, the need to re-examine critically the impact of the dominant orthodoxies of the international financial institutions on developing countries over the last few decades (see Mosley, 2000; Chang, 2002). Some very serious issues need to be acknowledged and confronted. They have been summarized pithily by Branko Milanovic in the form of three questions:

(i) How to explain that after sustained involvement and many structural adjustment loans, and as many IMF's Stand-bys, African GDP per capita has not budged from its level of 20 years ago? Moreover, in 24 African countries, GDP per capita is less than in 1975, and in 12 countries even below its 1960's level.

(ii) How to explain the recurrence of Latin crises, in countries such as Argentina, that months prior to the outbreak of the crisis are being praised as model reformers.

(iii) How to explain that . . . 'pupils' among the transition countries (Moldova, Georgia, Kyrghyz Republic, Armenia) after setting out in 1991 with no debt at all, and following all the prescriptions of the IFIs, find themselves 10 years later with their GDPs halved and in need of debt-forgiveness. (2003, p. 679)

Something is clearly awry. The dominant economic orthodoxies have not succeeded in many parts of the developing world; they have failed to generate sustained economic growth, poverty reduction and fair outcomes.

3

The Regulation of Economic Globalization: A New Policy Mix

A social democratic agenda which addressed the issues laid out above would be an agenda which meets the social democratic tests specified earlier (see p. 17). These focus policy explicitly on the promotion and deepening of the rule of international law, the pursuit of greater transparency, accountability and democracy in global governance, a renewed commitment to social justice, particularly focused on the least advantaged and the least well-off, the provision of the necessary public goods for the regulation and sustainability of the global economy, and the promotion of the engagement of leading stakeholders in corporate governance.

It is possible to distinguish broadly between a narrow economic agenda – most commonly referred to as the Washington consensus – and a social democratic vision of the reform of global economic processes. The narrow agenda is focused typically on free trade, capital market liberalization, flexible exchange rates, market-determined interest rates, the deregulation of all markets, the transfer of assets from the public to the private sector, the tight focus of public expenditure on well-directed social targets, balanced budgets, tax reform, secure property rights and the protection of intellectual property rights. It has been the dominant orthodoxy over the last twenty years in leading OECD countries, and in the international financial institutions.[1] Although elements of this orthodoxy

[1] The term 'Washington consensus' in the economic and development literatures is broadly associated with these policy recommendations. They were first set out authoritatively by John Williamson (although without direct reference to free capital mobility) (1990). Critics charge that these measures are bound up

rightly retain a place in a social democratic framework, the latter is distinguished by being tough in pursuit of free markets while insisting on a framework of shared values and common institutional practices, that is, a balance of open markets, strong governance, social protection and distributive justice at the global level. A progressive economic agenda needs to calibrate the freeing of markets with poverty reduction programmes and the immediate protection of the vulnerable – north, south, east and west.

If globalization is to mean not just global market integration but also global social integration and a commitment to social justice, then a social democratic agenda needs to be concerned with the promotion of those core values and principles which affirm that each and every person is treated, in principle, with equal concern and respect. This amounts to the promotion of a set of internationalist or cosmopolitan values, from the sanctity of life to a diversity of human rights, that attach to every human being, irrespective of where he or she was born or brought up. And it involves the promotion of these values and principles in regional and global governance. In case it be thought that these values and principles are for another world – for future times and not the present – it needs to be remembered that they are at the core of the 1948 UN Declaration of Human Rights and subsequent 1966 Covenants on Rights which raised them to a universal reference point: the requirement that all individuals be treated with equal concern and respect, irrespective of the state in which they were born or brought up, is the central pillar of the human rights worldview, and of a wide range of international treaties that have been agreed under UN auspices (see Held, 2002; and

---

with US geopolitics, that all too often they are preached by the US to the rest of the world but not practised by it, and that they are deeply destructive of the social cohesion of the poorest countries (see, most recently, Stiglitz, 2002, 2003a). Williamson has responded to some of his critics by arguing that his policy recommendations are sensible principles of economic practice, whoever recommends and deploys them, and that they leave open the question of the progressivity of the tax system (1993). The point at issue here will be that while some of the policies of the Washington consensus may be reasonable in their own terms, they represent too narrow a set of policies to help create sustained and equitable development and growth.

part III below). Anchored in this postwar legacy, global social democracy aims to combine a universal focus with policies that address the most pressing cases of harm and need. This can be thought of as *targeted egalitarianism* (Kelly, 2002), addressing the marginal and excluded while seeking to ensure that globalization works for all.

Economic growth can provide a powerful impetus to the achievement of human development targets. But it does not necessarily achieve these targets; unregulated economic development which simply follows existing rules and entrenched interests falls short of managed economic change geared to the prosperity of all. Economic development needs to be conceived as a means to an end, not an end in itself. Understood accordingly, it should be recognized that while international trade has huge potential for helping the least well-off people and countries to lift themselves out of poverty, and for enhancing the welfare and well-being of all nation-states, the current rules of global trade are heavily structured to protect the interests of the well-off and are heavily stacked against the interests of the poorest countries (see Oxfam, 2002; Moore, 2003).

According to the World Bank, abolishing all trade barriers could boost global income by $2.8 trillion and lift 320 million people out of poverty by 2015 (World Bank, 2001). In principle, this could cut global poverty by a quarter, which represents the equivalent of lifting out of poverty the very poorest in sub-Saharan Africa. If the WTO's Doha round, which was started in January 2002, achieved even half of this objective, it would be a major step forward. In this respect, the breakdown of talks at Cancún in September 2003 should not be allowed to deflect the 146 countries of the WTO from the urgency of establishing a new agreement. The coalition of developing countries (the G21) led with growing confidence by Brazil, India and China provided a much needed counterweight to the massive bargaining power of the EU and the US, and should be wholeheartedly welcomed. In the long run, it can be hoped, this coalition will help ensure that any future trade agreement preserves the focus on eradicating the trade rules, regulations and forms of protectionism that most handicap developing countries.

However, while free trade is an admirable objective for progressives in principle, it cannot be pursued without attention to the poorest in the least well-off countries who are extremely vulnerable to the initial phasing in of external market integration (especially of capital market liberalization), and who have few resources, if any, to fall back on during times of economic transformation (see Legrain, 2002; Garrett, forthcoming). The same is true, of course, for many people in wealthier societies. If they lose their jobs or have to settle for lower wages, they are also vulnerable in times of major economic shifts. In other words, a single-minded concern with 'market access' issues is, as the previous chapter indicated, insufficient.

It is thus crucial to any social democratic agenda for free markets that it addresses simultaneously the needs of the most vulnerable wherever they are. This will mean in developed countries the continued enhancement of robust, accountable political institutions to help mediate and manage the economic forces of globalization, and the provision of, among other things, high levels of social protection and generous safety nets, alongside sustained investment in lifelong learning and skills acquisition (cf. Swank, 2002a). For the poorest countries this will mean that development policies must be directed to ensure the sequencing of global market integration, particularly of capital markets, long-term investment in health care, human capital and physical infrastructure, and the development of transparent, accountable political institutions. What follows here is complex and challenging for every country. But what is striking is that this range of policies has all too often not been pursued. This seems more a matter of psychology and political choice, and less a matter related to any fundamental obstacles in the nature of the economic organization of human affairs.

A more detailed social democratic agenda for economic globalization and global economic governance follows. Each element would make a significant contribution to the creation of a level playing field in the global economy; together, they would help shape an economic system that was both free and fair. The agenda is set out under a number of core headings:

Trade

Creating impartial rule systems and market access

1   The pursuit of impartial, rule-based free trade through the current round of trade negotiations is urgent. The trade round begun at Doha needs to be a successful development round – one that brings real benefits to poor countries and the least well-off.

2   Access to developed markets for developing countries needs to be decisively improved, involving, at a minimum, the removal of quotas on textiles and clothing by the agreed deadline of 2005, and the tighter application of the rules governing anti-dumping measures (see Bhagwati, 2002).

3   Agricultural subsidies in all OECD countries need to be phased out.[2] This includes the fundamental reform of the Common Agricultural Policy (CAP), leading to the eventual abolition of domestic and export subsidies for EU agricultural products.[3] And it includes the huge subsidies of the US cotton industry and other agricultural sectors. Tariff escalating mechanisms which discriminate against developing countries when they add value to farmed products, among other goods, also need to be removed.

4   All subsidies that harm poor producers and provide perverse economic incentives leading to the unsustainable use of natural resources need to be removed over time.

5   The reform, if not outright abolition, of the Trade-Related Aspects of Intellectual Property Rights (TRIPS) Agreement

[2]   The numbers are alarming. As Stiglitz has pointed out: 'subsidies in advanced countries exceed the total income of sub-Saharan Africa; the average European subsidy per cow matches the $2 per day poverty level on which billions of people barely subsist; America's $4 billion cotton subsidies to 25,000 well-off farmers bring misery to 10 million African farmers' (2003b, p. 14).

[3]   The abolition of the CAP may require transitory financial support for those poor countries that have come to depend on subsidized agricultural products from the EU.

is critical.[4] At the minimum, there should be an end to the universal application of the WTO intellectual property blueprint, with developing countries enjoying the right to maintain short-term and more flexible systems of intellectual property protection; there must be a clear and continuing commitment to put public health priorities before the claims of patent holders, building on commitments made at the Doha ministerial conference in 2001 and more recently at Cancún; and there must be a prohibition on patent protection for genetic resources for food and agriculture, along with stronger rights for poor countries to develop more appropriate forms of plant-related protection, and protection of farmers' rights to save, sell and exchange seeds. In addition, the option to enforce TRIPS by imposing trade sanctions should be removed (see Oxfam, 2002, p. 16).

6 The creation of an international knowledge bank to help defray the costs of the use of patents, where they are already established and where particular knowledge-related inventions are vital for development purposes, is a pressing consideration (see Stiglitz, 1999).

7 A more balanced liberalization agenda needs to be achieved by addressing not just goods and services but also temporary labour flows, including of unskilled labour. A relatively small programme of increasing temporary work visas in the developed countries could generate substantial income gains for workers from the poorest countries. Indeed, it has been estimated that such gains might even exceed the predictions for income gains for all of the proposed Doha reforms (see Rodrik, 2003).

8 Strengthening the capacity of developing countries to participate more effectively in international trade negotiations,

---

[4] TRIPS raises the price of all know-how and technology, especially in poor countries: patented rice that poor farmers plant, copyrighted textbooks that poor students need, patented software that poor businessmen use are all examples of the ways in which TRIPS currently works to increase the price of knowledge-related goods for development purposes. I am indebted to Phillipe Legrain for clarifying these issues.

including at the WTO, is an important additional step. Many of the poorest countries have no permanent representation at the WTO headquarters in Geneva, and programmes which enhance their representative capacity are urgent. Initiatives like the WTO legal advisory centre need to be built on.

9   The promotion of good governance at all levels of economic activity – that is, the establishment of transparent public services, the protection of commercial activity from corruption, the rule of law and the maintenance of relevant property rights, alongside accountable and replaceable politicians – needs to be nurtured to ensure that markets eventually work without political, bureaucratic and corrupt impediment.

10 There needs to be an improvement in the transport and support infrastructures of developing countries so that they can export more. Transport costs, for example, can often be a serious barrier to trade, and a better transport infrastructure can help in the expansion of trade.

11 The possible establishment of a social chapter or social clause in the core provisions of the WTO should be explored.[5] This could provide a means (to be reinforced by other measures) to ban forced and child labour, to enforce trade union freedom, collective bargaining and the right to strike, and to eliminate, in principle, all forms of work-based discrimination. The point of such a social clause would not be to erode the competitive advantages of developing and transition economies on a comparative cost basis, but rather to build into the free trade system itself the necessary requirements for free trade to be fair in relation to minimum social and trade union conditions (see below and chapter 9).

---

[5]   The first substantive paragraph of the Agreement Establishing the WTO contains a precedent for this by placing priority on ensuring that the expansion of trade is consistent with raising standards of living and sustainable development. See http://www.wto.org/english/docs e/legal e/final e.htm. The consistency of trading arrangements with environmental protection is taken up in chapter 9.

Aid

Establishing short-term funds for investment
in human infrastructure (health, education, etc.)
and internal integration

1   All developed countries must adopt legally binding minimum
levels of overseas development assistance if there is to be
adequate investment in the internal integration of the poorest countries. All developed countries should be called on to
set a clear timetable for reaching the UN's 0.7 per cent of
GNP target for overseas aid. In addition, aid should be
refocused on poverty reduction in countries with particularly
low income. At present, too much of global aid is spent
on middle income countries at the expense of the poorest
nations. More aid resources should be linked to direct support
for developing countries' own poverty reduction strategies.

2   Governments should agree to untie their aid budgets so that
developing countries can strengthen their own procurements
systems and purchase goods and services from the most cost
effective source.[6]

3   A radical reduction in the international debt burden borne
by the 'heavily indebted poor countries' (HIPC) is also
necessary to ensure that debt levels are brought down to
sustainable levels. Despite numerous debt relief initiatives by
the World Bank, the IMF and other agencies, debt remains
a burden preventing poorer countries from generating consistent economic growth. Every dollar the West gives in aid
to developing countries is still met by several dollars return-
ing in the form of debt servicing (see Hertz, 2004).

4   A reduction in debt levels and debt servicing could be linked
to a system that encourages, for example, families to send

---

[6]   The untying of aid in this way should not be confused with relinquishing all
conditionality in relation to such funds – conditionality linked to the practices of
good governance including the transparent and accountable use of funds, zero
corruption, the direct payment of aid to targeted organizations, and so on.

their children to school by compensating them directly for the loss of a child's income (Roy, 2003). It has been estimated that the cost of getting 4 million children back to school for one year in Brazil is equivalent to just over 1 per cent of that country's 1998 debt servicing repayments. Extending such a programme to 10 million children between the ages of six and ten would cost just over 3 per cent of debt servicing payments. In other words, a direct link could be made between the reduction of debt servicing commitments, of debt overall, and the funding of children in schools. Other possibilities include linking such reductions to basic health provision or infrastructural investments.

5 An international poverty line needs to be established that has a clearly defined threshold of income (including the value of income in kind). Such a line should be subject to a demonstrable scientific consensus and directly linked to future aid programmes. The UN and other principal international agencies need to establish a clear monitoring system for measuring the success or failure of anti-poverty policies in meeting this standard.

New revenue streams

Securing new redistributive mechanisms
for long-term investment in the essential
conditions of human development – sanitation,
health, education, etc.

1 The creation of an international finance facility is indispensable to help meet internationally agreed poverty reduction targets and, in the first instance, the UN's agreed Millennium Development Goals (see table 4). A model for such a facility has been set out by the UK Treasury in association with the UK Department for International Development (see HM Treasury, 2003). The aims of the facility are inspired by the world's commitment to tackling illiteracy, disease, poverty and underdevelopment in the world's poorest countries. Its

Table 4   UN Millennium Development Goals, 1999–2015

1   Eradicate extreme poverty and hunger:
   • reduce by half the proportion of people living on less than one dollar a day
   • reduce by half the proportion of people who suffer from hunger
2   Achieve universal primary education:
   • ensure that boys and girls complete a full course of primary schooling
3   Promote gender equality and empower women:
   • eliminate gender disparity in primary and secondary education preferably by 2005, and at all levels by 2015
4   Reduce child mortality:
   • reduce by two-thirds the mortality rate among children under five
5   Improve maternal health:
   • reduce by three-quarters the maternal mortality ratio
6   Combat HIV/AIDS, malaria and other diseases:
   • halt and begin to reverse the spread of HIV/AIDS
   • halt and begin to reverse the incidence of malaria and other major diseases
7   Ensure environmental sustainability:
   • integrate the principles of sustainable development into country policies and programmes; reverse loss of environmental resources
   • reduce by half the proportion of people without sustainable access to safe drinking water
   • achieve significant improvement in the lives of at least 100 million slum dwellers by 2020
8   Develop a global partnership for development:
   • develop further an open trading and financial system that is rule-based and non-discriminatory. Includes a commitment to good governance, development and poverty reduction – nationally and internationally
   • address the least developed countries' special needs. This includes tariff- and quota-free access for their exports; enhanced debt relief for heavily indebted poor countries; cancellation of official bilateral debt; and more generous official development assistance for countries committed to poverty reduction
   • address the special needs of landlocked and small island developing states

Table 4 *(continued)*

- deal comprehensively with developing countries' debt problems through national and international measures to make debt sustainable in the long term
- in cooperation with the developing countries, develop decent and productive work for youth
- in cooperation with pharmaceutical companies, provide access to affordable essential drugs in developing countries
- in cooperation with the private sector, make available the benefits of new technologies – especially information and communications technologies

founding principle is long-term funding guaranteed to the poorest countries by the richest as a supplement to national aid development programmes. The funding would be conditional on efforts to fight corruption, improve public financial management, encourage investment and develop further country-owned poverty reduction strategies.

2   In the longer run, a new transfer system has to be established within and across national communities to allow resources to be generated to alleviate the most pressing cases of avoidable economic suffering and harm. While such a system can be partially built on the model of the finance facility suggested above, it has to have a more durable foundation in the long term. Just as national governance requires a national taxation system to ensure adequate resources for public goods, so a similar fundraising and distributive system is required at the global level to ensure the means exist to alleviate systematically the conditions of the least well-off. New instruments are needed to create new forms of regional and global taxation – for instance, a consumption tax on energy use, or a tax on carbon emissions, or a global tax on the extraction of resources within national territories, or a tax on the GNP of countries above a certain level of development, or a transaction tax on the volume of financial turnover in foreign exchange markets. The ultimate purpose of such measures is the creation of independent (non-national) funds

which could be established to meet the most extreme cases of need. Sustained social framework investment in the conditions of every human being's development (sanitation, health, housing, education and so on) could then follow on a routine and regular basis.

Financial governance arrangements

Ensuring transparency, accountability and democracy

1   If the phased opening of markets to global trade is important to the successful integration of a country into the world economic system, the phased opening of financial markets is critical. This is especially true in relation to portfolio capital investment, where there are strong grounds, indicated in chapter 1, to be cautious about the benefits of global integration.[7] In addition to a sound framework of macroeconomic management, the development of a country's capacity for governance with respect to domestic financial markets should be a key element of its overall economic strategy. The enhancement of financial transparency, the control of corruption, the maintenance of the rule of law and the development of financial supervisory capacity have all to be pursued by a country if it is to integrate itself successfully into global financial markets in the long term. In many cases, this will require that developing countries are given both technical and financial assistance to create the necessary institutions.

2   Developing countries require greater access to, and an enhanced participatory role in, the core institutions of global financial governance. The arguments against giving

---

[7]   As one authoritative analyst has noted, 'the weight of evidence and the force of logic point . . . towards restraints on capital flows. It is time to shift the burden of proof from those who oppose to those who favor liberated capital' (Bhagwati, 1998, p. 12).

developing countries such access are weak.[8] The World Bank and the IMF are much less reliant now on wealthy country contributions than they were when they were initially founded. As repayments of existing loans constitute a significant proportion of the World Bank's income, the case for developed countries' dominance of the World Bank board and other institutions of global financial governance has weakened (Griffith-Jones, 2003). A range of institutional innovations are, accordingly, essential, from altering the ways in which leaders are selected for the World Bank and the IMF to increasing the voting shares of developing countries in their boards. Developing countries are underrepresented in international financial institutions. It is also essential to expand significantly the participation of developing countries in the Bank for International Settlements. Important progress was made in this regard in the 1990s, but significantly more remains to be achieved.

3   Developing countries, in addition, need to be included in the crucial financial fora from which they are currently excluded, including the Financial Stability Forum (FSF) (which only grants access to Singapore and Hong Kong). At the present time, developing countries have no voice in some key international financial organizations, and this despite the fact that decisions are taken there that affect them significantly. One proposal in this regard suggests that developing countries could be included in the FSF and Basel

---

[8]   It could be argued that good domestic governance (economic and political) should be made a condition for increasing a developing country's weight in global economic institutions. Such an argument carries considerable appeal, and is consistent with the importance placed on transparency, accountability and democracy throughout this book; it would give developing countries an additional incentive for the reform of their institutions, where these suffer from corruption, authoritarianism and so on. However, this argument should be considered cautiously since the democratic reform of institutions (at all levels) takes a considerable time to put in place and to become effective. And the arguments for preserving the current dominance of developed countries in global economic institutions are now, as will be seen, thin. Moreover, unless the voices of developing countries are strengthened in global economic institutions, it seems highly improbable that the development agenda will be given the urgent attention it requires.

Committee on a rotational basis, which would not substantially increase the size of these groups and, therefore, not put at risk their effective working practices. An example of this might be two representatives per developing country region (Latin America, Asia and Africa) who might be nominated for two years and then rotated (Griffith-Jones, 2003).

4 Attention must be focused on improving cooperation among international financial institutions and other international donors, thus consolidating the policy-making efforts of the international community with regard to financial governance within the UN system. At the moment, institutional arrangements and divisions too often lead to initiatives which conflict or undermine each other. For example, mandates vary, jurisdictions conflict, responsibilities overlap, and even the geographic location of some of the core international financial organizations are based on Cold War considerations which are now out of date.

5 The world's current financial institutions were created more than fifty years ago in an economic context that has drastically changed. At best, these institutions are no longer self-evidently equipped to deal with the challenges that many countries face, and accordingly their mandates and briefs should be reassessed. At worst, they have often been responsible for compounding the problems they sought to resolve, and they should be radically overhauled, if not disbanded (Stiglitz, 2002; Held and Koenig-Archibugi, 2003). There should be a substantial review of the functioning of the Bretton Woods institutions. Such a review should include a re-examination of the framework for structural adjustment programmes with a different range of conditionality, linking the latter to wider social justice considerations (poverty and equity impacts); a change in the capital quotas in the IMF and World Bank with a view to their more equitable distribution; the establishment of a world financial authority to monitor and supervise global financial markets and capital flows (see Eatwell and Taylor, 2000); and new or reinforced regional financial institutions with a mandate to serve more local needs.

MNCs

Embedding corporations in rules to help ensure
'good practices' and multistakeholder dialogue

1 The corporate coverage of the UN's Global Compact (GC)
   should be extended and deepened, with a view to the
   engagement of companies in the promotion of core UN
   principles (see table 5). The overall objective should be to
   encourage companies to move towards 'good practices' as
   defined through the maintenance of these principles and
   multistakeholder dialogue and partnership about their
   implementation (see chapter 9).
2 The creation of a code of conduct for MNCs, which would
   be voluntary in the first instance, and would build on the
   principles and regulatory rules laid down in the GC.[9]
3 In the long term governments should aim to create a legally
   binding international protocol, based on the GC principles,
   to govern the production, trade and consumption of all
   resources (see Oxfam, 2002).
4 The development of a global anti-trust mechanism is another
   element that needs to be stressed. In the light of the concentration of corporate power in the global economy today, it
   is necessary to extend the principles of anti-monopoly legislation found within national borders to the wider global
   economy.

The policy objectives set out above, and the underlying reasons
for them, provide a rationale for a politics of intervention in
economic life – not to control and regulate markets for their own

---

[9] While bringing MNCs into a global compact of this kind is desirable, it needs
to be noted that many abuses associated with them are often linked to their
subcontractors. Moreover, it is frequently the case that MNCs pay higher wages,
provide better working conditions and have higher environmental standards than
many more local firms. In addition, most people do not work for MNCs and a
global compact needs to address the behaviour and activities of domestic firms
as well.

Table 5 Core UN principles for the Global Compact

The core principles are:
- support and respect for the protection of internationally proclaimed human rights
- non-complicity in human rights abuses
- freedom of association and the effective recognition of the right to collective bargaining
- the elimination of all forms of forced and compulsory labour
- the effective abolition of child labour
- the elimination of discrimination in respect of employment and occupation
- a precautionary approach to environmental challenges
- greater environmental responsibility, and
- the encouragement of the development and diffusion of environmentally friendly technologies

Source: Ruggie, 2003, p. 126

sake, but to provide the basis for a free, fair and just world economy, and to ensure that the values of efficient and effective global economic processes are compatible with the agenda of social democratic values. The roots of such necessary intervention lie in the indeterminacy of the market system itself (see Sen, 1985). Markets work, but not always, not perfectly and not necessarily reliably (Kay, 2003a). Market economies can only function in a manner commensurate with self-determination, democracy, human rights and environmental sustainability if this indeterminacy is addressed systematically and if the conditions of social democratic governance are met, in the short and long term.

Part II
POLITICS

4

Political Globalization

Economic globalization has not occurred in a static political system; there has been a shift in the nature and form of political organization as well. A distinctive aspect of this is the emergence of 'global politics' (McGrew, 1992). Political events in one part of the world can rapidly acquire worldwide ramifications. Spatially focused political activity, whether in a city or subnational region, can become embedded in extensive networks of political interaction. As a result, developments at the local level – whether economic, social or environmental – can acquire almost instantaneous global consequences and vice versa (Giddens, 1990, ch. 2).

The new context of politics

Nations, peoples and social movements are linked by many new forms of communication. Over the last few decades a wave of new technological innovations, along with the transformation of older technologies, has generated global communication and transportation infrastructures. These have opened up a massive series of communication channels that cross national borders, increasing the range and type of communications to and from all the world's regions. In addition, contemporary patterns of communication have created a far greater intensity of concepts, symbols and images, moving with far greater extensity and at a far greater velocity, than in earlier periods. This process is compounded by the fact that new global communication systems are used for business and

73

commercial purposes. While there remain significant differences in information density and velocity in different parts of the globe, it is becoming increasingly difficult for people to live in any place isolated from the wider world.

These developments have engendered fundamental changes in the organization of political life. The close connection between 'physical setting', 'social situation' and politics which distinguished most political associations from premodern to modern times has been ruptured; the new communication systems create new experiences, new modes of understanding and new frames of political reference independently of direct contact with particular peoples, issues or events. The speed with which the events of 9/11 reverberated across the world and made mass terrorism a global issue is one poignant example.

The idea of global politics calls into question the traditional demarcations between the domestic and the foreign, and between the territorial and the non-territorial, found in modern conceptions of 'the political' (see Held et al., 1999, chs 1, 2 and 8). These categories shaped not only modern political thought but also institution building, as a clear division was established between great ministries of state founded to focus on domestic matters and those created to pursue geopolitical questions. Global problems highlight the richness and complexity of the interconnections that now transcend states and societies in the global order. Moreover, global politics is anchored today not just in traditional geopolitical concerns – trade, power, security – but in a large diversity of social and ecological questions. Pollution, water supply, genetically engineered food and drugs are among an increasing number of policy issues which cut across territorial jurisdictions and existing political alignments, and which require international cooperation for their satisfactory resolution. In many parts of the world the notion of global politics corresponds much more closely to the character of politics than do images of politics as simply state and interstate relations (Keohane and Nye, 2000). There are now multiple spheres of politics and authority.

In charting political globalization, it is important to explore the way in which the sovereign state is now criss-crossed by a vast array of networks and organizations that have been established to regulate and manage diverse areas of international and transnational activity – trade, communications, crime and so on. The rapid growth of transnational issues and challenges has generated a multicentric system of governance both within and across political borders (Rosenau, 2002). It has been marked by the transformation of aspects of territorially based political decision-making, the development of regional and global organizations and, in many places, the increased importance of regional and international law. There is nothing inevitable, it should be stressed, about these developments. While they form highly significant trends, they are contingent upon many factors, and could be halted or reversed by protracted global conflicts or cataclysmic events (see Keohane and Nye, 2000).

Multicentric governance

In the first instance, where once states were the main actors, and multilateral international conventions, negotiated over many years, were the primary expression of interstate cooperation, today this constitutes too narrow a view of international politics. For the primary actors in the international order are no longer just heads of states and foreign ministries, but administrative agencies, courts and legislatures as well (Slaughter, 2003b). The unitary state has given way to the 'disaggregated state' and the rise of government networks. While these networks take many forms and perform a variety of different functions, they herald 'a new era of transgovernmental regulatory co-operation' and define transgovernmentalism 'as a distinctive mode of global governance: horizontal rather than vertical, composed of national government officials rather than international bureaucrats, decentralized and informal rather than organized and rigid' (Slaughter, 2003b, p. 190). Influential examples include the networks formed by financial regulators, including central bankers, securities regulators, insurance supervisors and anti-trust officials. Regulatory networks are a key medium for adjusting and responding to the fast moving challenges of the information age; and through them political power is recast – not simply eroded or undermined.

The end of the Cold War and of the division of the world by two superpowers marks a new distribution of power among states, markets and civil society. New information technologies have helped drive the expansion of networks of businesses, citizens, trade unions, IGOs and INGOs (international non-governmental organizations) which now share aspects of power with governments. The hierarchical organization of governments is increasingly ill-equipped to manage and regulate the new divisions of economic, social and cultural resources. Although it is not easy to imagine political entities that could compete with 'the emotional attachment of a shared landscape, national history, language, flag, and currency', new geographic and functional entities are emerging which challenge the state's hegemony in these areas (Mathews, 2003; Kaldor, 2003). The development of global cities, such as London, Barcelona and Los Angeles, substate regions (Catalonia, Scotland, Quebec) and new political formations like the EU, alongside the explosive growth of INGOs and social movements, creates new forms of hybrid organization and allegiances. These networks of business, INGOs and IGOs solve problems, from economic management to environmental tasks, that governments cannot resolve alone. Despite the resurgence of US power and unilateralist politics since 9/11, this underlying transformation of power is likely to continue (see Raustiala, 1997).

The development of new forms of political and regulatory bodies can be illustrated by a number of phenomena, including, most obviously, the rapid emergence of multilateral organizations and transnational agencies. New forms of multilateral and global politics have been established involving governments, IGOs, INGOs, and a wide variety of pressure groups and other non-governmental organizations (NGOs). At the start of the twentieth century there were just a handful of IGOs and INGOs; by 1996 there were 4,667 active IGOs and 25,260 active INGOs (UIA, 2002). Membership in organizations of this sort has increased across all income country categories, even though, not surprisingly, the nature and extent of membership varies considerably across such categories and by region (see figures 5–7). In addition, there has been a very substantial development in the number of international treaties in force, as well as in the number of international

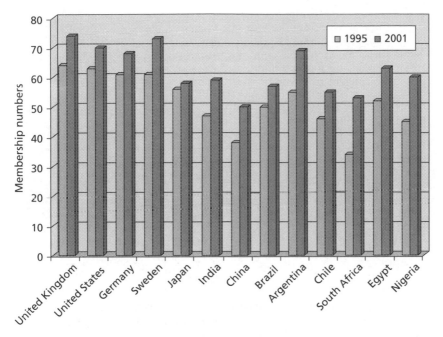

Figure 5 Membership of selected countries in formal multilateral organizations, 1995 and 2001
Source: The Foreign Policy–A. T. Kearney Globalization Index, at www.foreignpolicy.com/wwwboard/g-index.php

regimes, formal and informal, altering the political and legal context in which states operate (Held et al., 1999, chs 1–2).

To this dense web of political interconnectedness can be added the routine pattern of meetings and activities of the key international policy-making fora, including the UN, G7, IMF, World Bank and WTO. A century and a half ago there were just one or two interstate conferences or congresses per annum; today the number totals over 9,000 annually (UIA, 2002). National government is increasingly locked into an array of governance systems at diverse levels – and can barely monitor them all, let alone stay in command. Foreign and domestic policies have become chronically intermeshed, making the coordination and control of government policy increasingly complex.

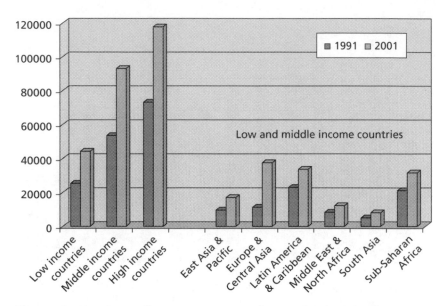

Figure 6 Numbers of non-governmental organizations having members in low income, middle income and high income countries, and by region, 1991 and 2001
Source: Anheier, Glasius and Kaldor, 2002, pp. 324–8, using data from Union of International Associations (UIA, 2002), www.uia.org

A thickening web of multilateral agreements, institutions, regimes and transgovernmental policy networks has evolved over the last five decades, intervening in and regulating many aspects of national and transnational life, from finance to flora and fauna.[1] This evolving global governance complex is, of course, far from constituting a world government, with ultimate legal authority and coercive powers, but it is much more than a system of limited intergovernmental cooperation. With the UN as its institutional core, it comprises a vast range of formal suprastate bodies and regional organizations (see figure 8), as well as regimes and transnational policy networks embracing government officials, technocrats,

---

[1] The following three paragraphs are adapted from material in Held and McGrew, 2002b, pp. 59–71.

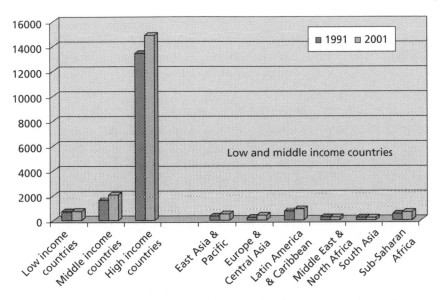

Figure 7 Number and geographic spread of the secretariats of international and internationally oriented non-governmental organizations
Source: Anheier, Glasius and Kaldor, 2002, p. 322, using data from Union of International Associations (UIA, 2002), www.uia.org

corporate representatives, pressure groups and non-governmental organizations. Although these bodies and networks lack the kind of centralized, coordinated political programme that is associated with national government, few would dismiss out of hand the expanding jurisdiction or scope of global policy-making, most especially the vast range of issues it touches on (see table 6) and its growing intrusion into the domestic affairs of states – illustrated, for example, by the rulings of the WTO's trade dispute panels. Whatever its limits and faults, the current system of global governance is a significant arena 'in which struggles over wealth, power and knowledge are taking place' (see Murphy, 2000).

Global governance today is a *multilayered*, *multidimensional* and *multi-actor* system. It is multilayered in so far as the development and implementation of global policies involve a process of political coordination between suprastate, transnational, national

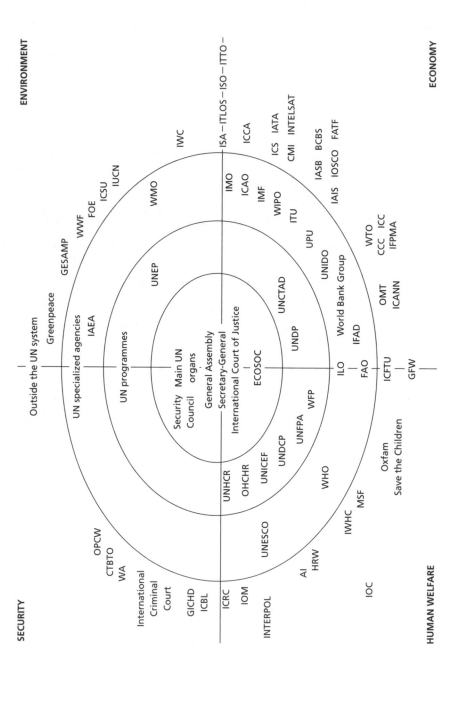

SECURITY

ENVIRONMENT

HUMAN WELFARE

ECONOMY

Outside the UN system

Greenpeace

UN specialized agencies

UN programmes

Security Main UN
Council   organs

General Assembly

Secretary-General

International Court of Justice

ECOSOC

GESAMP

WWF

FOE

ICSU

IUCN

IWC

ISA – ITLOS – ISO – ITTO –

ICCA

ICS   IATA

CMI   INTELSAT

IASB   BCBS

IAIS   IOSCO   FATF

IMO

ICAO

IMF

WIPO

ITU

UPU

UNIDO

World Bank Group

WTO

CCC   ICC

IFPMA

OMT

ICANN

IFAD

ILO

FAO

ICFTU

GFW

WMO

UNEP

IAEA

UNCTAD

UNDP

WFP

UNFPA

UNDCP

UNICEF

OHCHR

UNHCR

WHO

MSF

IWHC

Oxfam

Save the Children

IOC

AI

HRW

UNESCO

INTERPOL

IOM

ICRC

ICBL

GICHD

International
Criminal
Court

WA

CTBTO

OPCW

Key to abbreviations

AI	Amnesty International
BCBS	Basel Committee on Banking Supervision
CCC	Customs Cooperation Council
CMI	Comité Maritime International
CTBTO	Comprehensive Nuclear-Test-Ban Treaty Organization (not yet operational)
ECOSOC	UN Economic and Social Council
FAO	Food and Agriculture Organization
FATF	Financial Action Task Force
FOE	Friends of the Earth
GESAMP	Joint Group of Experts on the Scientific Aspects of Marine Environmental Protection
GFW	Global Fund for Women
GICHD	Geneva International Centre for Humanitarian Demining
HRW	Human Rights Watch
IAEA	International Atomic Energy Agency
IAIS	International Association of Insurance Supervisors
IASB	International Accounting Standards Board
IATA	International Association of Transport Airlines
ICANN	Internet Corporation for Assigned Names and Numbers
ICAO	International Civil Aviation Organization
ICBL	International Campaign to Ban Landmines
ICC	International Chamber of Commerce
ICCA	International Council of Chemical Associations
ICFTU	International Confederation of Free Trade Unions
ICRC	International Committee of the Red Cross
ICS	International Chamber of Shipping
ICSU	International Council for Science
IFAD	International Fund for Agricultural Development
IFPMA	International Federation of Pharmaceutical Manufacturers Associations
ILO	International Labour Organization
IMF	International Monetary Fund
IMO	International Maritime Organization
INTELSAT	International Telecommunications Satellites Organization
INTERPOL	International Criminal Police Organization
IOC	International Olympic Committee
IOM	International Organization for Migration
IOSCO	International Organization of Securities Commissions
ISA	International Seabed Authority
ISO	International Organization for Standardization
ITLOS	International Tribunal for the Law of the Sea
ITTO	International Tropical Timber Organization
ITU	International Telecommunication Union
IUCN	World Conservation Union
IWC	International Whaling Commission
IWHC	International Women's Health Coalition
MSF	Médecins Sans Frontières
OHCHR	Office of the High Commissioner for Human Rights
OMT	World Tourism Organization
OPCW	Organization for the Prohibition of Chemical Weapons
UNCTAD	UN Conference on Trade and Development
UNDCP	UN Drug Control Programme
UNDP	UN Development Programme
UNEP	UN Environment Programme
UNESCO	UN Educational, Scientific and Cultural Organization
UNFPA	UN Population Fund
UNHCR	UN High Commissioner for Refugees
UNICEF	UN Children's Fund
UNIDO	UN Industrial Development Organization
UPU	Universal Postal Union
WA	Wassenaar Arrangement on Export Controls for Conventional Arms and Dual-Use Goods and Technologies
WFP	World Food Programme
WHO	World Health Organization
WIPO	World Intellectual Property Organization
WMO	World Meteorological Organization
WTO	World Trade Organization
WWF	Worldwide Fund for Nature

Figure 8 The organizational infrastructure of global governance: a UN-centric view
Source: Koenig-Archibugi, 2002

Table 6 Major intergovernmental bodies

Issue	*Governance institutions*
Economic	
Trade	WTO; EU regional trade agreements
Growth/macrostability	G8; OECD; IMF; tax treaties
Investment flows	Bilateral investment agreements (BITs)
Services	BITs; WTO (GATS)
Intellectual property rights	WTO (TRIPS); WIPO
Financial stability	G8; IMF; Basel Bank for International Settlements
Corruption	OECD Bribery Convention; UN Convention on Corruption
Money laundering	IMF
Competition policy/ restrictive practices	European Commission; UNCTAD; bilateral information sharing agreements
Travel/tourism	IMO; ICAO; WTO (tourism)
International communications	ITU; UPU; WTO
International product standards	International Standards Organisation; Codex Alimentarius
Social	
Human rights; torture	UN – UN Commission for Human Rights; ICC
Labour rights	ILO; UNCTAD
Health	WHO; ILO; UNAIDs
Development; poverty reduction	World Bank; UNDP; UNIDO; FAO; bilateral donors
Refugees	UN High Commissioner for Refugees
Humanitarian assistance	UN World Food Programme; bilateral donors
Genocide/crimes against humanity/war crimes	ICC; UN tribunals for Rwanda and former Yugoslavia
Transboundary crime	Interpol; UNDCP; UNICRI; UN Commission on Narcotic Drugs; UN Commission on Crime Prevention and Criminal Justice
Landmines	Ottawa Landmines Convention
Education/culture	UNESCO
Environmental	
Climate change/ozone	UNFCCC; Kyoto Protocol; GEF; Montreal Protocol

Table 6   (*continued*)

Issue	Governance institutions
Natural resources	FAO; UNCLOS; CSD; 217 MEAs
Biodiversity	CBD; CITES; Ramsar Convention on Wetlands
Waste/toxics	Basel Convention on Hazardous Waste; London Dumping Convention
Space	Moon Treaty
Antarctica	Antarctic Convention
Security	
State aggression	UN Security Council; NATO
Conflict prevention/ resolution	UN Security Council
Terrorism	Interpol
Energy security	International Energy Agency
WMD non-proliferation	UN; IAEA; CTBTO; OPCW

Source: UK Government, Prime Minister's Strategy Unit

and often substate agencies. Attempts to combat AIDS/HIV, for instance, require the coordinated efforts of global, regional, national and local agencies. It is multidimensional in so far as the engagement and configuration of agencies often differs from sector to sector and issue to issue, giving rise to significantly differentiated political patterns. The politics of, for example, global financial regulation is different in interesting ways from the politics of global trade regulation. Further, many of the agencies of, and participants in, the global governance complex are no longer purely intergovernmental bodies. There is involvement by representatives of transnational civil society – from Greenpeace to Jubilee 2000 and an array of NGOs; the corporate sector – from Monsanto to the International Chamber of Commerce and other trade or industrial associations; and mixed public–private organizations, such as the International Organization of Security Commissions (IOSCO). Accordingly, global governance is a multi-actor complex in which diverse agencies participate in the development of global public policy. Of course, this essentially pluralistic conception of global governance does not presume that all states or interests have an equal voice in, let alone an equal influence over, its agenda or programmes – not at all.

An important feature of the formulation and implementation of global public policy is that it occurs within an expanding array of different kinds of networks – transgovernmental networks (such as the Financial Action Task Force (FATF)), trisectoral networks (such as the World Commission on Dams Forum), involving public, corporate and NGO groups, and transnational networks (such as the International Accounting Standards Board (IASB)) (McGrew, 2002b). These networks – which can be ad hoc or institutional – have become increasingly important in coordinating the work of experts and functionaries within governments, international organizations and the corporate and the NGO sectors. They function to set policy agendas, disseminate information, formulate rules and establish and implement policy programmes – from the money-laundering measures of the FATF to global initiatives to counter AIDS. While many of these networks have a clear bureaucratic function, they have also become mechanisms through which civil society and corporate interests are embedded in the global policy process (examples include the Global Water Partnership and the Global Alliance for Vaccines and Immunization). In part, the growth of these networks is a response to the overload and politicization of multilateral bodies, but it is also an outcome of the growing technical complexity of global policy issues and the communications revolution.

Another notable trend is the growing enmeshment of public and private agencies in the making of rules, the setting of codes and the establishment of standards. Many new sites of rule-making and lawmaking have emerged, creating a multitude of 'decentred lawmaking processes' in various sectors of the global order (Teubner, 1997, p. xiii). Many of these have come into existence through processes of self-validation in relation to technical standardization, professional rule production and transnational regulation of multinational corporations, and through business contracting, arbitration and other elements of *lex mercatoria* (the global framework of commercial law) (see Teubner, 1997). A new transnational legal order is developing, 'globalizing a corpus of commercial law and practice that derives from increasingly diverse and multiple local, regional, and global locations involving both state and nonstate authorities' (Cutler, 2003, p. 3). Global public policy networks are reshaping the basis on which national and international rules are made and regulatory systems operate; and the results cannot easily be fitted into traditional legal distinctions (Jayasuriya, 1999; Reinicke, 1999). There is no longer a strict separation between public and private, domestic and international legal procedures and mechanisms; models of lawmaking and enforcement no longer simply follow the form and logic of the states system.

To this complex pattern of global governance and rule-making can be added the new configurations of regional governance. The EU has, in remarkably little time, taken Europe from the edge of catastrophe in two world wars to a world in which sovereignty is pooled across a growing number of areas of common concern. For all its flaws, it is, judged in the context of the history of states, a remarkable political formation. In addition, there has been a significant acceleration in regional relations beyond Europe: in the Americas, in Asia-Pacific and, to a lesser degree, in Africa. While the form taken by this type of regionalism is very different from the model of the EU, it has nonetheless had significant consequences for political power, particularly in the Asia-Pacific, which has seen the formation of ASEAN, APEC, ARF, PBEC, and many other groupings (see Payne, 2003). Furthermore, as regionalism has deepened, so interregional diplomacy has intensified as old and new regional groups seek to consolidate their relations with each other. In this respect, regionalism, as noted earlier, has not been a barrier to globalization; it has been a building block for it (see Hettne, 1998).

Interlaced with these political and legal transformations are changes in the world military order; a key consideration for the argument being made here. Few states, except for the US and China, can now realistically contemplate unilateralism or neutrality as a credible defence strategy. Global and regional security institutions have become more significant as the collectivization of national security has evolved (Clarke, 2001). But it is not just the institutions of defence that have become multinational. The way military hardware is manufactured has also changed. The age of 'national champions' has been superseded by a sharp increase in licensing co-production agreements, joint ventures, corporate alliances and subcontracting (Held et al., 1999, ch. 2). This means that few countries – not even the United States – can claim to have a wholly autonomous military production capacity. Such a point can be highlighted in connection with key civil technologies, such as electronics, which are vital to advanced weapons systems, and which are themselves the products of highly globalized industries.

The paradox and novelty of the globalization of organized violence is that security today is increasingly a collective or multilateral affair. The war against Iraq in 2003 occupies an interesting place in this regard. While the dominant military position of the US allows it to act unilaterally – indeed, two weeks before the start of the war, the US Secretary of Defense, Donald Rumsfeld, made it clear to the British government that the US was willing and able to act alone – it has been unable to protect its soldiers after the formal declaration of the end of hostilities, and unable to win the peace. At the time of writing, the US is searching for multilateral support (from India, Japan and other countries) in the form of both military and financial assistance; and it is hoping that a new resolution in the UN (resolution 1511, 16 October 2003) will help restore legitimacy to its control of Iraq and release further international resources. While the war dramatized the military power of the US and its willingness to deploy this massive capability, it also highlighted how complex security challenges and threats cannot be managed satisfactorily by states acting alone, or even in small alliances.

Moreover, states no longer have a monopoly of force, as the growth of transnational terrorism and the events of postwar Iraq all too clearly demonstrate. Private armies and the private provision of security also play a significant role in many regions of the globe. Thus, for the first time in history, the one thing that did most to give modern nation-states a focus and a purpose, that is, national security, and that has been at the very heart of modern statehood as understood from Hobbes onwards, can now be realized effectively only if nation-states come together and pool resources, technology, intelligence, power and authority.

The reconfiguration of political power

Political communities can no longer be considered (if they ever could with any validity) as simply 'discrete worlds'; they are enmeshed in complex structures of overlapping forces, relations and networks. Clearly, these are structured by inequality and hierarchy. However, even the most powerful among them – including the most powerful states – do not remain unaffected by the changing conditions and processes of regional and global entrenchment.

At the core of these developments is the reconfiguration of political power (Held et al., 1999, Conclusion). While many states retain the ultimate legal claim to effective supremacy over what occurs within their own territories, this should be juxtaposed with, and understood in relation to, the expanding jurisdiction of institutions of global and regional governance and the constraints of, as well as the obligations derived from, new and changing forms of international regulation (see chapter 6). This is especially evident in the European Union, where sovereign power is divided between international, national and local authorities, but it is also evident in the operation of IGOs such as the WTO (Moore, 2003). However, even where sovereignty still appears intact, states do not retain sole command of what transpires within their own territorial boundaries. Complex global systems, from the financial to the ecological, connect the fate of communities in one locale to the fate of communities in distant regions of the world. Globalization, in other words, is associated with a transformation or an 'unbundling' of the relationship between sovereignty, territoriality and political power (Ruggie, 1993; Sassen, 1996).

This unbundling involves a plurality of actors, a variety of political processes, and diverse levels of coordination and operation. Specifically, it includes:

- Different forms of intergovernmental arrangements embodying various levels of legalization, types of instruments utilized and degrees of responsiveness to stakeholders.
- An increasing number of public agencies – such as central bankers – maintaining links with similar agencies in other

countries and thus forming transgovernmental networks for the management of various global issues.

- Diverse business actors – for instance, firms, their associations and organizations such as international chambers of commerce – establishing their own transnational regulatory mechanisms to manage issues of common concern.
- Non-governmental organizations and transnational advocacy networks – that is, leading actors in global civil society – playing a role in various domains of global governance and at various stages of the global public policy-making process.
- Public bodies, business actors and NGOs collaborating in many issue areas in order to provide novel approaches to social problems through multistakeholder networks.

While many people – politicians, political activists and academics – link contemporary globalization with new constraints on politics, it is more accurately associated with the expansion of the terms of political activity. Not only has contemporary globalization triggered or reinforced the significant politicization of a growing array of issue areas, it has been accompanied by an extraordinary growth of institutionalized arenas and networks of political mobilization, decision-making and regulatory activity which transcend national political jurisdictions. This has expanded the capacity for, and scope of, political activity and the exercise of political authority. In principle, globalization is not beyond regulation and control. Yet it is hard to overlook the profound institutional and normative challenges it presents to the existing organization of political communities.

5

Globalization and the Challenges to Governance

Contemporary globalization embodies elements in common with past phases, but it is distinguished by some unique organizational features, creating a world shaped increasingly by new technologies, the global economy, the development of regional and global governance structures, new forms of international regulation, and the creation of global systemic problems – growing global inequalities, market volatility, money laundering, the international drugs trade, mass terrorism, global warming and AIDS, among other phenomena. Some striking challenges to the nature and form of governance are posed by these developments.

First, contemporary processes of globalization and regionalization create overlapping networks of interaction and power. These cut across territorial boundaries, putting pressure on, and straining, a world order designed in accordance with the principle of exclusive sovereign rule over a delimited territory. One consequence of this is that the locus of effective political power is no longer simply that of national governments; effective power is shared, bartered and contested by diverse forces and agencies, public and private, crossing national, regional and international domains.

Against the background of dense networks of global interaction, the power of even the greatest states can come to depend on cooperation with others for its effective execution. Few recent developments illustrate this better than the war on terrorism led by the US. The fight against terrorism depends not just on the sharing of military intelligence, hardware and personnel around the world, but also on the capacity of the US to win the fight for 'the hearts and minds' of people in many regions, some of whom currently see the US as a self-interested bastion of privilege and arrogance (see Nye, 2002). Without addressing this latter battle, the US will in all likelihood achieve, at best, only partial victories.

We are, as Kant most eloquently put it over two hundred years ago, 'unavoidably side by side'. However, in a world where powerful actors and forces cut across the boundaries of national communities in diverse ways, and where the decisions and actions of leading states can ramify across the world, the questions of who should be accountable to whom, and on what basis, do not easily resolve themselves.

The second challenge to governance concerns the development of two regulatory gaps which weaken political institutions, national and international (Kaul, Grunberg and Stern, 1999, pp. xixff.). These are:

- a jurisdictional gap – the discrepancy between national, separate units of policy-making and a regionalized and globalized world, giving rise to the problem of externalities such as market volatility or the degradation of the global commons, the problem of who is responsible for them, and how they can be held to account; and
- an incentive gap – the challenge posed by the fact that, in the absence of any supranational entity to regulate the supply of global public goods, many states and non-state actors will seek to free ride and/or lack sufficient motivation to find durable solutions to pressing transnational problems.

While governance in the global order involves multilayered, multidimensional and multi-actor processes in which institutions and politics matter a great deal to the determination of policy outcomes, these are distorted generally in favour of leading states and vested interests (see Keohane, 2003b). Hence, for example, despite the vociferous dissent of many protest groups in recent years, the promotion of the global market has taken clear priority over many pressing environmental and social issues, and in agriculture and textiles in particular the protected markets of developed countries have remained in place.

It is a troubling fact that while nearly 3,000 people died on 9/11, almost 30,000 children under five die each day in the developing world from preventable diseases, diseases which have been practically eradicated in the West. Such overwhelming disparities in life chances are not found only in the area of health, but are reproduced across almost every single indicator of global development. The third challenge to governance emerges from a reflection on this and involves what might be called a 'moral gap'; that is, a gap defined by:

1 a world in which, as indicated earlier, over 1.2 billion people live on less than a dollar a day, 46 per cent of the world's population live on less than 2 dollars a day, and 20 per cent of the world's population enjoy over 80 per cent of its income; and

2 by commitments and values often shaped by 'passive indifference' to the many consequences of this for the poorest in the world, illustrated by UN expenditure per annum of $1.25 billion (plus peacekeeping) compared with US confectionery expenditure of $27 billion per annum, US alcohol expenditure of $70 billion per annum, and US expenditure on cars of $550 billion per annum (US Economic Census, 1997, at www.census.gov/epcd/www/econ97.html).

This is not an anti-America statement, of course. Equivalent EU figures could have been highlighted.

Among the political difficulties produced by these interlocking challenges (regulatory and moral) is a growing imbalance in global rule-making and enforcement. As Ruggie put it,

those rules that favor global market expansion have become more robust and enforceable in the last decade or two – intellectual property rights, for example, or trade dispute resolution through the World Trade Organization. But rules intended to promote equally valid social objectives, be they labour standards, human rights, environmental quality or poverty reduction, lag behind and in some instances actually have become weaker. One result is the situation where considerations of patent rights have trumped fundamental human rights and even pandemic threats to human life . . . (2003, pp. 96–7).

That global systems of rules and inequalities spark conflict and contestation can hardly be a surprise, especially given the visibility of the world's lifestyles in an age of mass media. How others live is now generally known to us, and how we live is generally known to them.

Fourth, while there has been a shift from relatively distinct national communication and economic systems to their more complex and diverse enmeshment at regional and global levels, and from government to multilevel governance, there are few grounds for thinking that a parallel 'globalization' of political identities has taken place (Held et al., 1999, ch. 7). One exception to this is to be found among the elites of the global order – the networks of experts and specialists, senior administrative personnel and transnational business executives – and those who track and contest their activities, the loose constellation of social movements (including the anti-globalization movement), trade unionists and (a few) politicians and intellectuals. But these groups are not typical. Thus we live with a challenging paradox – that governance is becoming increasingly a multilevel, intricately institutionalized and spatially dispersed activity, while representation, loyalty and identity remain stubbornly rooted in traditional ethnic, regional and national communities (Wallace, 1999). One important qualification can usefully be added to this point: while those who have a commitment to the global order as a whole and to international institutions are a distinct minority, a generational divide is evident. Those born after the Second World War are more likely to see themselves as cosmopolitans, to support the UN system and lend their support to the free trade system and the free movement of migrants. Age cohort analysis indicates that over the long term public opinion is moving in a more international direction (Norris, 2000). Recent findings from the Pew Global Attitudes Project confirm this trend: despite the youthful nature of the anti-globalization movement, it found that young people in most West European and Latin American countries are more positive about globalization than their elders, and that young people in most of the world are enthusiastic about increased global communications and cultural flows (see www.people-press.org). Of course, it remains to be seen whether this tendency crystallizes into a clearly focused political orientation.

Hence, the shift from government to multilayered governance, from national economies to economic globalization, is a potentially unstable shift, capable of reversal in some respects and certainly capable of engendering a fierce reaction – a reaction drawing on nostalgia, romanticized conceptions of political community, hostility to outsiders (refugees), a search for a pure national state (as in the politics of Le Pen in France), and the restatement of unsullied, fundamentalist beliefs and ideals. But this reaction itself is likely to be highly unstable, and perhaps a relatively short- or medium-term phenomenon. To understand why this is so, nationalism has to be disaggregated.

As 'cultural nationalism' it is, and in all probability will remain, central to people's identity; however, as 'political nationalism' – the assertion of the exclusive political priority of national identity and the national interest – it may not remain as significant; for political nationalism cannot deliver many sought-after public goods without seeking accommodation with others, in and through regional and global collaboration. In this respect, only an international or cosmopolitan orientation can, ultimately, meet the political challenges of a more global era, marked by overlapping communities of fate and multilevel/multilayered politics.

6

The Reform of Global Governance

Problem solving at the global level is marked by a number of difficulties. In the first instance, there is no clear division of labour among the myriad of international governmental agencies; functions often overlap, mandates frequently conflict, and aims and objectives too often get blurred. There are a number of competing and overlapping organizations and institutions all of which have some stake in shaping global public policy. As one observer has noted in relation to global social policy (Deacon, 2003), the fragmentation and competition that takes place is between:

- the World Bank, IMF, WTO and the UN system;
- the UN Secretariat and UN social agencies;
- the G7, G20 and G77 and other groupings of countries; and
- a host of national social initiatives.

The World Bank's health and social policies are not the same as those of the World Health Organization (WHO), UNESCO or the International Labour Organization, to name but some bodies. The United Nations Secretary-General's initiatives, such as those involving the Millennium Project (see table 5 above), are not necessarily the same as, and are in some tension with, the social policies of the UN's Department of Economic and Social Affairs and the aims of the UN Development Programme (UNDP) and WHO. While the G7 often has a set of reasonably clear global policy objectives, these are typically in conflict with the G20 and the G77 (the coalition of southern, developing countries), the latter often seeking to form an opposition grouping to the agenda of the G7 (see Deacon, 2003).

Reflecting on the difficulties of interagency cooperation during his time as head of the WTO, Mike Moore has written that 'greater coherence amongst the numerous agencies that receive billions of taxpayers' dollars would be a good start . . . this lack of coherence damages their collective credibility, frustrates their donors and owners and gives rise to public cynicism . . . the array of institutions is bewildering . . . our interdependent world has yet to find the mechanism to integrate its common needs' (2003, pp. 220–3).

A second set of difficulties relates to the inertia found in the system of international agencies, or the inability of these agencies to mount collective problem-solving solutions faced with disagreement over means, objectives, costs and so on. This often leads to a situation where the cost of inaction is greater than the cost of taking action. For the reform of the world trade regime and the treatment of serious diseases which threaten many countries it has been estimated that the costs of inaction are about one hundred times greater than the costs of corrective action (see Conceição, 2003). The failure to act decisively in the face of urgent global problems can not only compound the costs of dealing with these problems in the long run, but also reinforce a widespread perception that these agencies are not just ineffective but unaccountable.

The perceived accountability deficit is linked to two interrelated difficulties: the power imbalances among states, as well as those between state and non-state actors in the shaping and making of global public policy. Multilateral bodies need to be fully representative of the states involved in them, and they rarely are. In addition, there must be arrangements in place to engage in dialogue and consultation between state and non-state actors, and these conditions are only partially met in multilateral decision-making bodies. Investigating this problem, Inge Kaul and her associates at the UNDP have made the telling point that 'the imbalances among states as well as those between state and non-state actors are not always easy to detect, because in many cases the problem is not merely a quantitative issue – whether all parties have a seat at the negotiating table. The main problem is often qualitative – how well various stakeholders are represented' (Kaul et al., 2003, p. 30).

Having a seat at the negotiating table in a major IGO or at a major conference does not ensure effective representation. For even if there is parity of formal representation, it is often the case that developed countries have large delegations equipped with extensive negotiating and technical expertise, while poorer developing countries often depend on one-person delegations, or even have to rely on the sharing of a delegate. Moreover,

> a one person delegation today does not necessarily have the same negotiating strengths as a one person delegation several years ago. The negotiating load has increased: the international policy agenda is lengthening, issues are becoming more complex, organizations are multiplying, conference venues are being shifted from continent to continent, meetings are being held in parallel sessions, and 'informal informals' are becoming a common negotiating tool. (Kaul et al., 2003, p. 31)

All of these issues stretch the capacities of small negotiating delegations to the limit. The difficulties that occur range from the significant underrepresentation of developing countries in agencies such as the IMF – where twenty-four industrial countries hold ten to eleven seats on the executive board while forty-two African countries hold only two – to problems that result from an inability to develop substantial enough negotiating and technical expertise even with 'one person one country' decision-making procedures (see Buira, 2003; Chasek and Rajamani, 2003; Mendoza, 2003). Accordingly, many people are stakeholders in global political problems that affect them, but remain excluded from the political institutions and strategies needed to address these problems.[1]

An additional problem emerges as a result of issues which span the distinction between the domestic and the foreign. A growing number of issues can be characterized as 'intermestic' – that is, issues which cross the international and domestic (Rosenau, 2002). These are often insufficiently understood, comprehended or acted

[1] There were interesting signs at the September 2003 trade discussions at Cancún that leading developing countries are beginning to learn from these problems and combine expertise and negotiating resources.

on. For there is a fundamental lack of ownership of global problems at the global level (Moore, 2003, p. 218). It is far from clear which global public issues are the responsibility of which international agencies. The institutional fragmentation and competition leads not just to the problem of overlapping jurisdictions among agencies, but also to the problem of issues falling between agencies. This latter problem is also manifest between the global level and national governments. The time has come – to say the very least – to examine these matters again.

Underlying these institutional difficulties is the breakdown of symmetry and congruence, referred to earlier, between decision-makers and decision-takers (p. 13). The point has been well articulated recently by Kaul and her associates in their work on global public goods. They speak about the forgotten *equivalence* principle (see Kaul et al., 2003, pp. 27–8). This principle suggests that the span of a good's benefits and costs should be matched with the span of the jurisdiction in which decisions are taken about that good. At its simplest, the principle suggests that those who are significantly affected by a global good or bad should have a say in its provision or regulation. Yet all too often there is a breakdown of 'equivalence' between decision-makers and decision-takers, between decision-makers and stakeholders, and between the inputs and outputs of the decision-making process. As a result, we face the challenge of:

- *Matching circles of stakeholders and decision-makers* – to create opportunities for all to have a say about global public goods that affect their lives.
- *Systematizing the financing of global public goods* – to get incentives right and to secure adequate private and public resources for these goods.
- *Spanning borders, sectors, and groups of actors* – to foster institutional interaction and create space for policy entrepreneurship and strategic issue management. (Kaul et al., 2003, pp. 5–6)

Failures or inadequacies in global political processes often result from the mismatch between the decision-making circles created in international arenas, and the range of spillovers associated with specific public goods or public bads. 'The challenge is to align the circles of those to be consulted (or to take part in the decision making) with the spillover range of the good under negotiation' (Kaul et al., 2003, p. 28).

Traditionally, the tension between the sphere of decision-makers and the sphere of decision-takers has been resolved by the idea of political community – the bounded, territorially delimited community in which decision-makers and decision-takers create processes and institutions to resolve the problem of accountability. During the period in which nation-states were being forged – and the territorially bound conception of democracy was consolidated – the idea of a close mesh between geography, political power and democracy could be assumed. It seemed compelling that political power, sovereignty, democracy and citizenship were simply and appropriately bounded by a delimited territorial space. These links were by and large taken for granted and generally unexplicated (Held, 1995). But they no longer can be. Globalization, global governance and global challenges raise issues concerning the proper scope of democracy, and of a democracy's jurisdiction, given that the relation between decision-makers and decision-takers is not necessarily symmetrical or congruent with respect to territory.

The principle of inclusiveness and subsidiarity is often regarded in democratic theory as a helpful means to clarify the fundamental criterion for drawing proper boundaries around those who should be involved in particular decision-making domains and those who should be accountable to a particular group of people (see Held, 1996). At its simplest, it states that those significantly (that is, non-trivially) affected by public decisions, issues or processes should, *ceteris paribus*, have an equal opportunity, directly or indirectly through elected delegates or representatives, to influence and shape them. Those affected by public decisions ought to have a say in their making (see Whelan, 1983; Saward, 2000).

While this principle points in an important direction, it is only in association with the idea of a political community that it is compelling; for here decision-makers and decision-takers meet by convention to resolve matters of common fate. But the issue is:

how is the notion of 'significantly affected' to be understood when the relation between decision-makers and decision-takers is more spatially complex – when, that is, decisions affect people outside a circumscribed democratic entity? To take some examples: A decision to permit the 'harvesting' of rainforests may contribute to ecological damage far beyond the borders that formally limit the responsibility of a given set of decision-makers. A decision to build a nuclear plant near the frontiers of a neighbouring country is a decision likely to be taken without consulting those in the nearby country (or countries) despite the many risks for them. A decision by large US corporations such as IBM or Microsoft can have profound effects on the economic opportunities in countries such as India, but it will in all likelihood be taken without consultation with those in far-off lands.[2] In these situations, as Robert Keohane put it, 'the normative question arises . . . should the acting entity be accountable to the set of people it affects? . . . Merely being affected cannot be sufficient to create a valid claim. If it were, virtually nothing could ever be done, since there would be so many requirements for consultation and even veto points' (2003b, p. 141).

This is a hard issue to resolve. The issue becomes a little easier to think through if the all-affected principle is connected directly to the idea of impact on people's needs or interests. If we think of the impact of powerful forces on people's lives, then impact can be divided into three categories: strong, moderate and weak. By strong I mean that vital needs or interests are affected (from health to housing), with fundamental consequences for people's life expectancy. By moderate I mean that needs are affected in such a way that people's ability to participate in their community (in economic, cultural and political activities) is in question. At stake here is the quality of life chances. By weak I mean an effect which has an impact on particular lifestyles or the range of available consumption choices (from clothes to music). These categories are not watertight and require further theoretical analysis (cf. Doyal and Gough, 1991; Held, 1995), but they provide some useful guidance:

---

[2] Other examples include the decision to go to war. War raises exceptional questions, aspects of which I return to in part III.

- If people's urgent needs are unmet, their lives will be in danger. In this context, people are at risk of serious harm.
- If people's secondary needs are unmet, they will not be able to participate fully in their communities and their potential for involvement in public and private life will remain unfulfilled. Their choices will be restricted or depleted. In this context, people are at risk of harm to their life opportunities.
- If people's lifestyle needs are unmet, their ability to develop their lives and express themselves through diverse media will be thwarted. In this context, unmet need can lead to frustration. (Frustration could be thought of as a weak term, but it can give rise to serious tension and conflict.)

In the light of these considerations, the principle of inclusiveness and subsidiarity needs restating. I take it to mean here that those whose life expectancy and life chances are significantly affected by social forces and processes ought to have a stake in the determination of the conditions and regulation of these, either directly or indirectly through political representatives. Democracy is best located when it is closest to and involves those whose life expectancy and life chances are determined by powerful entities, bringing the circles of stakeholders and decision-makers closer together. The argument for extending this consideration to decisions and processes which affect lifestyle needs is less compelling, since these are fundamentally questions of value and identity for communities to resolve for themselves. Whether McDonald's should be allowed access across China, or US media products given free range in Canada, are questions largely for those countries to resolve, although clearly serious cross-border issues concerning, for example, the clash of values and consumption choices can develop, posing questions about regional or global trade rules and regulations.

The principle of inclusiveness and subsidiarity points to the necessity of both the decentralization *and* the centralization of political power. If decision-making is decentralized as much as possible, it maximizes the opportunity of each person to influence the social conditions that shape his or her life. But if the decisions at issue are translocal, transnational or transregional, then political institutions need not only to be locally based but also to have a wider scope and framework of operation. In this context, the creation of diverse sites and levels of democratic fora may be unavoidable. It may be unavoidable, paradoxically, for the very same reasons as decentralization is desirable: it creates the possibility of including people who are significantly affected by a political issue in the public (in this case, transcommunity public) sphere. If diverse peoples beyond borders are effectively stakeholders in the operation of select regional and global forces, their de facto status as members of diverse communities would need to be matched by a de jure political status, if the mechanisms and institutions that govern these political spaces are to be brought under the rubric of the principle of inclusiveness and subsidiarity. Stakeholders in de facto communities and networks of local, national, regional and global processes will be politically empowered only if they achieve the necessary complementary de jure status.

Properly understood, the principle of inclusiveness and subsidiarity should be taken to entail that decision-making should be decentralized as much as possible, maximizing each person's opportunity to influence the social conditions that shape his or her life. Concomitantly, centralization is favoured if, and only if, it is the necessary basis for avoiding the exclusion of persons who are significantly affected by a political decision or outcome (Pogge, 1994, pp. 106–9). These considerations yield, as one analyst has written, 'the result that the authority to make decisions of some particular kind should rest with the democratic political process of a unit that (1) is as small as possible but still (2) includes as equals all persons significantly . . . affected by decisions of this kind' (Pogge, 1994, p. 109).

Elsewhere, I have proposed three tests to help filter policy issues to different levels of democratic governance: the tests of extensity, intensity and comparative efficiency (Held, 1995, ch. 10). The test of extensity assesses the range of people within and across borders whose life expectancy and life chances are significantly affected by a collective problem and policy question. The test of intensity examines the degree to which the latter impinges on a group of people(s) and, therefore, the degree to which regional or global initiatives are warranted. The third test – the test of comparative efficiency – is concerned to provide a means of examining whether any proposed regional or global initiative is necessary in so far as the objectives it seeks to meet cannot be realized satisfactorily by those working at 'lower' levels of local or national decision-making.[3] Accordingly, the principle of inclusiveness and subsidiarity may require diverse and multiple democratic public fora for its suitable enactment. It yields the possibility of multilevel democratic governance. The ideal number of appropriate democratic jurisdictions cannot be assumed to be embraced by just one level – as it is in the theory of the liberal democratic nation-state (Held, 1996, part 2).

Strengthening global governance

To restore symmetry and congruence between decision-makers and decision-takers, and to entrench the principle of equivalence in a manner that is consistent with inclusiveness and subsidiarity, requires a strengthening of global governance and a resolve to address those challenges previously discussed – institutional competition, overlapping jurisdictions, the excessive costs of inaction, etc. In the first instance, this agenda can be thought of as comprising three interrelated dimensions:

- promoting coordinated state action to tackle common problems;
- reinforcing those international institutions that can function effectively;
- developing multilateral rules and procedures that lock in all powers, small and major, into a multilateral framework (see Hirst and Thompson, 2002, pp. 252–3).

Such a strategy means promoting intergovernmentalism and inter-state action to tackle problems like international criminal networks

---

[3] The criteria that can be used to pursue an inquiry into comparative efficiency include the availability of alternative local and national legislative or administrative means, the cost of a proposed action and the possible consequences of such action for the constituent parts of an area (see Neunreither, 1993).

and the containment of new epidemics; adopting the widest possible strategies for intergovernmental and interstate consultation and coalition building; recognizing the necessary role of the international financial institutions while reforming their governance structures; and strengthening IGO capacity (particularly that of the ILO) to negotiate new and enforce existing conventions on core labour standards, migration and international labour mobility. This strategy amounts to a policy of creating an enlightened multilateralism, built on the principles of extending open markets, strong coordinated governance, and providing protection against social vulnerabilities wherever possible. It amounts to an initial attempt to specify the meaning of social democracy at the global level. But it can only be regarded as a first approximation – ambitious as it is in the current political climate (see Hirst and Thompson, 2002).

Systematizing the provision of global public goods requires not just building on existing forms of multilateral institutions, but also on extending and developing them in order to address questions of inadequate provision, accountability and democracy. A programme in this regard has been set out recently by the UNDP. It affirms the necessity of developing a number of new global institutional tools to foster both the supply of public goods and the public nature of decision-making about them. The following recommendations are made:

- promoting the principle of stakeholder-decisionmaker equivalence;
- developing criteria for fair negotiations;
- strengthening the negotiating capacity of developing countries;
- developing rules for interactions between state and non-state actors;
- creating advisory scientific panels for all major global issues, following the example of the Intergovernmental Panel on Climate Change;
- creating negotiating arenas for new priority issues (such as the right of access to water for all people), together with appropriate grievance panels (such as a world water court);
- creating demand-driven review and response facilities to promote flexible implementation of policy regimes, such as

a trade and development review council within the World
Trade Organization. (Kaul et al., 2003, p. 49)

The programme represents an imaginative leap forward in the
thinking about how to provide global public goods in a framework of public involvement.

Jean-François Rischard has also recently stressed that the current international system is simply not effective, accountable or
fast enough to solve many of the big global issues we face – issues
set out earlier under the headings of those concerning our planet,
our humanity and our rule-book (see table 1, p. 12 above). In this
regard, he argues that the creation of major treaties is typically
too slow a process, and often leads to legal agreements and instruments that are not enforced; big UN conferences are helpful at
raising levels of awareness about a global issue, but often fail to
produce detailed solutions to those issues; G7/G8-type meetings
can be very productive but are mostly reactive to problems that
have occurred; and the world's leading IGOs, while they are sometimes quite effective, are rarely in a position to take a major initiative with regard to pressing global public problems (see Rischard,
2002, part 3). Rischard stresses too that it is not enough simply to
develop existing multilateral institutions, but that new innovative
solutions are required if the core political problems we face are to
have any hope of effective resolution within a legitimate framework of accountability. He is sceptical about our ability to create
new institutions soon enough to resolve pressing global issues,
and he is sceptical about the ability of such institutions to act
effectively in the short term. So against such notions, he proposes
global issues networks (GINs). He argues that what we require
is a distinct global issue network for each urgent policy problem.
What would this look like?

Rischard argues (2002, p. 171) that it is possible to conceive of
the development of a global issue network in three stages:

- a constitutional phase, when the network is convened and
  set in motion;
- a norm-producing phase, beginning with a rigorous evalu-
  ation of options and alternatives;

- an implementation phase, in which the network takes on a rating role, helping the norms exert their influence through reputation effects.

Such networks could be permanent or temporary and each would be charged with developing policy recommendations for core pressing problems, such as global warming, biodiversity and ecosystem losses. Each network would be initiated by a leading international actor working purely as a facilitator – not a problem solver in its own right. The GIN's membership would include representatives of governments concerned by and experienced in the issue at hand, as well as knowledgeable people from business and international non-governmental organizations. The GIN's brief would be to dissect a global problem and search for solutions. It would be asked to draw up detailed norms and standards which could, in principle, resolve the issue, and which could be used to put formal and informal pressure on the various players involved in the generation, and future solution, of the problem. The core phases in the development of global issue networks are set out in figure 9.

GINs would seek to set out new standards of behaviour required of key agents to solve global problems, and would then act as a kind of rating agency to expose countries, businesses or other players that were not living up to the new standards. For example, they would regularly 'name and shame' governments that had not passed legislation conforming to the standards, or had not ratified or enforced a perfectly useful treaty, or had not altered domestic policy where it mattered.

The creation of a global issue network is clearly, in principle, a very flexible instrument to help bypass or circumvent organizations that have insufficient clarity about the problem involved, confusing mandates or an inability to act decisively.[4] But there are

---

[4] It is interesting to note that the EU is exploring similar policy instruments through its 'open method of coordination'. In utilizing this method, member states agree to formulate national action plans in particular areas by drawing on their distinctive and common experiences, subjecting proposals to testing by a panel of expert officials drawn from a broad spectrum of member states, reviewing performance against relevant targets and considering various incentives, and sanctions if necessary, to ensure policy success (see Cohen and Sabel, 2003).

The constitutional phase

1 year

Each GIN enlists members from:
• Governments
• International civil society organizations
• Businesses

Facilitators:
• One global multilateral as lead facilitator
• One co-facilitator from civil society
• One co-facilitator from the business world

The norm-producing phase

[1 year +] 2–3 years

Methodology used by the GIN:
• Disciplines and substance, no posturing
• Deliberative polling through electronic town meetings (ETMs)
• Rough consensus

Substance of the GIN's work:
• What is the problem?
• How much time do we have?
• Where do we want to be twenty years from now?
• How do we want to get there?
• What are the options?
• What should the norms be?
   – Detailed norm packages
   – Other recommendations

The implementation phase

[1 year + 2–3 years] > 10 years

New tasks:
• Rating countries and players against norms
• Creating reputation effects through naming-and-shaming
• Observatory and knowledge-exchange roles

Figure 9 Global Issues Networks (GINs)
Source: Rischard, 2002, pp. 173, 175, 177

problems with this mechanism if it is used on its own. While the new networks are designed to put pressure on government organizations and agencies to perform better and more effectively, they contribute little to the question of norm and rule enforcement in the face of a reluctant actor – political, economic or social – that might refuse to come into line or which, by virtue of taking no action, could perpetuate and add to the core problem involved. Nor do they provide a solution to the problem of how one determines the range of legitimate voices or stakeholders that ought to be involved in a GIN, or how this matter can be effectively arbitrated. In this respect, it is helpful to think of GINs as a useful short-term mechanism in the creation and extension of an enlightened multilateralism, but as an insufficient mechanism alone to reshape global governance and entrench social democratic values.

The policy issues and suggestions discussed above lay out an agenda for thinking about the reform of global governance in the immediate future. But a social democratic agenda for global governance reform also needs to think about how the existing form of intergovernmentalism, with its overlapping jurisdictions and fragmented structures, can be developed and improved in the longer run. Here it is necessary to think more boldly about a new social democratic multilateralism. This is not, of course, a multilateralism that can be implemented in all respects in the immediate future. But setting it out helps set down paths and goals for public policy reform at the global level. With this in mind, the following section lays out an agenda for a robust social democratic multilateralism.

Social democratic multilateralism

Social democratic multilateralism must take as its starting point a world of 'overlapping communities of fate'. Recognizing the complex processes of an interconnected world, it ought to view certain issues – such as housing, education and policing – as appropriate for spatially delimited political spheres (the city, region or state), while seeing others – such as the environment, world health and global economic regulation – as requiring new, more extensive institutions to address them. Deliberative and decision-making centres beyond national territories are appropriately situated when the principles of inclusiveness, subsidiarity and equivalence can only be properly upheld in a transnational context; when those whose life expectancy and life chances are significantly affected by a public matter constitute a transnational grouping; and when 'lower' levels of decision-making cannot manage satisfactorily transnational or international policy questions. Of course, the boundaries demarcating different levels of governance will always be contested, as they are, for instance, in many local, subnational regional and national polities. Disputes about the appropriate jurisdiction for handling particular public issues will be complex and intensive; but better complex and intensive in a clear public framework than simply left to powerful geopolitical interests (dominant states) or market-based organizations to resolve them alone.

The possibility of a global social democratic polity must be linked to an expanding framework of states and agencies bound by the rule of law, democratic principles and human rights. How should this be understood from an institutional point of view? Initially, the possibility of a global social democratic polity could be enhanced if the UN system actually lived up to its Charter. Among other things, this would mean pursuing measures to implement key elements of the Conventions on rights, and enforcing the prohibition on the discretionary right to use force (see Falk, 1995). However, while each move in this direction would be helpful, it would still represent, at best, a move towards a very incomplete form of accountability and justice in global politics. For the dynamics and logic of the current hierarchical interstate system (with the US in pole position) would still be an immensely powerful force in global affairs; the massive disparities of power and asymmetries of resource in the global political economy would be left virtually unaddressed; ad hoc responses to pressing international and transnational issues would remain typical; and the 'gaps' emphasized earlier would remain unbridged (see chapter 5). As a result, the deeply embedded difficulties of the UN system would be unaddressed and unresolved: the susceptibility of the UN to the agendas of the most powerful states, the weaknesses of many of its enforcement operations (or lack of them altogether), the underfunding of its organizations, the continued dependency of its programmes on the financial support of a few major states, the inadequacies of the policing of many environmental regimes (regional and global) and so on.

Thus a global social democratic polity would need to establish an overarching network of democratic public fora, covering cities, nation-states, regions and the wider transnational order. It is possible to conceive of different types of political engagement on a continuum from the local to the global, with the local marked by direct and participatory processes, while larger domains with significant populations are progressively mediated by representative mechanisms. The possibilities of direct involvement in the public affairs of small communities are clearly much more extensive compared to those which exist in highly differentiated social, economic and political circumstances (see Held, 1996, chs 7 and 9; Beetham, 1993, pp. 55–73; Phillips, 1993, pp. 93–111). However, the simple juxtaposition of participatory with representative democracy is now in flux given developments in information technology, putting simultaneous two-way communication within reach of larger populations (Budge, 1993, pp. 136–55); stakeholder innovations in democratic representation, emphasizing the significance of the direct involvement of representatives of all major groupings affected by a public process, instead of all the possible individuals involved (Bernheim, 1985; Hutton, 2002); and new approaches in deliberative democracy which do not take citizens' preferences as simply given or pre-set and, instead, seek to create accessible fora for the examination of opinion about common problems (Cohen, 1989; Fishkin, 1991; Cohen and Sabel, 1997, 2003). The aim of such fora is to establish a deliberative process whose structure grounds 'an expectation of rationally acceptable results' (see Habermas, 1996). Such a process can be conceived in terms of diverse public spheres in which broad spectrums of views are considered, and collective judgements are arrived at, through deliberation – deliberation guided by the requirements of impartiality. Being impartial here means being open to, reasoning from, and assessing all points of view (especially those of people in urgent need); it does not mean simply following the precepts of self-interest, whether based on class, gender, ethnicity or nationality (see Barry, 1999; Held, 2002). Political decisions that meet the standards of impartiality are those that would be defensible in relation to all parties if they had participated as equal partners in public debate.[5]

Accordingly, a social democratic polity would seek the creation of an effective and representative deliberative, administrative and regulative capacity at global and regional levels to complement that at national and local levels. This would require the following.

(1) The formation of an authoritative assembly of all states and agencies – a reformed General Assembly of the United Nations, or a complement to it. The focus of a global assembly would be the examination of those pressing global problems which are at the heart of concerns about life expectancy and life chances – concerns, for instance, about health and disease, food supply and distribution, the debt burden of the developing world, the instability of the hundreds of billions of dollars that circulate the globe daily, global warming and the reduction of the risks of nuclear, chemical and biological warfare. Its task would be to lay down, in framework-setting law, the standards and institutions required to embed the rule of law, democratic principles, and the minimum

---

[5]   In order to meet this standard a number of particular tests can be pursued, including an assessment of whether all points of view have been taken into consideration; whether there are individuals in a position to impose on others in such a manner as would be unacceptable to the latter, or to the originator of the action (or inaction), if the roles were reversed; and whether all parties would be equally prepared to accept the outcome as fair and reasonable irrespective of the social positions they might occupy now or in the future (see Barry, 1989, pp. 372, 362–3). These concerns are not overambitious. As one commentator aptly explained: 'All the impartiality thesis says is that, if and when one raises questions regarding fundamental . . . standards, the court of appeal that one addresses is a court in which no particular individual, group, or country has *special* standing. Before the court, declaring "I like it", "it serves my country", and the like, is not decisive; principles must be defensible to anyone looking at the matter apart from his or her special attachments, from a larger, human perspective' (Hill, 1987, p. 132, quoted in Barry, 1995, pp. 226–7). Impartialist reasoning will not, of course, produce a simple deductive proof of the ideal set of principles and conditions which can overcome the deficiencies of the global economy or global political order; nor can it produce a deductive proof of the best or only moral principles that should guide institutional formation. Rather, it should be thought of as a heuristic device to test candidate rules, principles and standards, and their various forms of justification. Better the requirements of this heuristic device than simply asserting 'I want it', 'It's in the interests of my government.'

conditions for human agency to flourish (see part III below for an elaboration of this legal trajectory). Consistent with this would be the creation of institutional capacities to initiate attempts – through a Social and Economic Security Council – to alleviate crises of urgent need that generate immediate life and death considerations. If non-global levels of governance were to fail to protect people in these circumstances, a *raison d'être* would exist for direct global intervention. Of course, political decision-making and implementation should remain, everything else being equal, as much as possible with those who are primarily and most immediately affected by them, in line with the principle of inclusiveness and subsidiarity.

Agreement on the terms of reference of a global assembly would be difficult, to say the least, although there is no shortage of plausible schemes and models (see Archibugi, 1995; Held, 1995; Monbiot, 2003). Ultimately, its terms of reference and operating rules would need to command widespread agreement and, hence, ought to be generated in a stakeholder process of consensus building – a global constitutional convention – involving states, IGOs, INGOs, citizen groups and social movements. A global process of consultation and deliberation, organized at diverse levels, represents the best hope of creating a legitimate framework for accountable and sustainable global governance.[6]

---

[6]   Three core issues would need to be addressed: Who is to be represented, governments or citizens? What is to be the principle of representation, one state one vote, proportional representation, or a mixture of both? What are the proper scope and limits of action of a global assembly? These are demanding questions which admit of a number of sound theoretical answers. The case for each would have to be considered and weighed in the context of the diversity of interests which would be brought to a global constitutional convention, for example the inevitable differences that would emerge between the developed and developing countries on whether population size or economic strength or a mixture of both should count in the determination of the basis of representation. While the legitimacy and credibility of a new global assembly would depend on it being firmly grounded on the principle of consent and electoral inclusiveness, it is likely that any assembly in the foreseeable future would be constituted by compromises between theoretical ideals and practical constraints. Accordingly, rather than set out blueprints for the nature and form of a global assembly, it seems better to stress the importance of a legitimate process of consensus building in and through which these issues might be deliberated upon and settled.

(2) The creation where feasible of regional parliaments and governance structures (for example, in Latin America and Africa) and the enhancement of the role of such bodies where they already exist (the European Union) in order that their decisions become recognized and accepted as legitimate independent sources of regional and international regulation.

(3) The opening up of functional international governmental organizations (such as the WTO, IMF and World Bank) to public examination and agenda setting. Not only should such bodies be transparent in their activities, but they should be open to public scrutiny (on the basis perhaps of elected supervisory bodies, or functional deliberative fora, representative of the diverse interests in their constituencies), and accountable to regional and global assemblies (see the first two points above).

(4) The establishment, where IGOs are currently weak and/or lacking in enforcement capability, of new mechanisms and organizations, for instance in the areas of the environment and social affairs (see chapter 3). The creation of new global governance structures with responsibility for addressing poverty, welfare and related issues is vital to offset the power and influence of market-oriented agencies such as the WTO and IMF.

(5) The enhancement of the transparency and accountability of the organizations of national and transnational civil society, addressing the potentially disturbing effects of those who are able to 'shout the loudest' and of the lack of clarity about the terms of engagement of non-state actors with IGOs and other leading political bodies (see Edwards and Zadek, 2003). Experiments are necessary to find ways of improving the internal codes of conduct and modes of operation of non-state actors, on the one hand, and of advancing their capacity to be represented in IGOs and other leading political bodies preoccupied with global policy processes, on the other. Moreover, to avoid citizens of developed countries being unfairly represented twice in global politics (once through their governments and once through their NGOs) special attention and support needs to be given to enhance the role of NGOs from developing countries.

(6) The use of general referenda cutting across nations and nation-states at regional or global levels in the case of contested priorities concerning the implementation of core global concerns. These could involve many different kinds of referenda, including a cross-section of the public, and/or of targeted and significantly affected groups in a particular policy area, and/or of the policy-makers and legislators of national parliaments.

(7) The development of law enforcement and coercive capability, including peacekeeping and peace-making, to help deal with serious regional and global security threats (see chapters 7 and 9). It is necessary to meet the concern that, in the face of the pressing and violent challenges to fundamental human rights and priorities, 'covenants, without the sword, are but words' (Hobbes). Capabilities in this regard could be developed, for example, if a proportion of a nation-state's military were permanently seconded to a UN peacemaking force or if international enforcement capacities were increased by creating a permanent independent force recruited directly among individuals who volunteer from all countries, and who could be trained in an international military academy.

In the long term, global social democracy must involve the development of both independent political authority and administrative capacity at regional and global levels. It would not call for the diminution *per se* of state power and capacity across the globe. Rather, it would seek to entrench and develop political institutions at regional and global levels as a necessary supplement to those at the level of the state (cf. Doyle, 2000). This conception of politics is based on the recognition of the continuing significance of nation-states, while arguing for layers of governance to address broader and more global questions. The aim is to forge an accountable and responsive politics at local and national levels alongside the establishment of representative and deliberative assemblies in the wider global order; that is, a political order of transparent and democratic cities and nations as well as of regions and global networks.

The long-term institutional requirements of global social democracy include:

- Multilayered governance and diffused authority.
- A network of democratic fora from the local to the global.
- Enhancing the transparency, accountability and effectiveness of leading functional IGOs; and building new bodies of this type where there is demonstrable need for greater public coordination and administrative capacity.
- Improving the transparency, accountability and voice of non-state actors.
- Use of diverse forms of mechanisms to access public preferences, test their coherence and inform public will formation.
- Establishment of an effective, accountable, international police/military force for the last resort use of coercive power in defence of international humanitarian or cosmopolitan law.

Multilevel citizenship

Against this background, the basis of a new conception of citizenship can be disclosed – a citizenship based not on exclusive membership of a territorial community, but on general rules and principles which can be entrenched and drawn on in diverse settings. This conception relies on the availability and clarity of the principles of democracy and human rights. These principles create a framework for all persons to enjoy, in principle, equal freedom and equal participative opportunities. The meaning of citizenship shifts from membership in a community which bestows, for those who qualify, particular rights and duties, to an alternative principle of world order in which all persons have equivalent rights and duties in the cross-cutting spheres of decision-making which affect their vital needs and interests. It posits the idea of a global political order in which people can enjoy an equality of status with respect to the fundamental processes and institutions which govern their life expectancy and life chances. As a result, the opportunities for citizenship would be extended to cover all political communities in which people have a critical stake (see Held, 1995, ch. 12). Citizenship would become multilevel and multidimensional, while being anchored in common rules and principles.

Within this context, the elusive and puzzling meaning of global citizenship becomes a little clearer. Built on the fundamental rights and duties of all human beings, global citizenship underwrites the autonomy of each and every human being, and recognizes their capacity for self-governance at all levels of human affairs. Although this notion needs further clarification and unpacking, its leading features are already within our grasp. Today, if people are to be free and equal in the determination of the conditions that shape their lives, there must be an array of fora, from the city to global associations, in which they can hold decision-makers to account. If many contemporary forms of power are to become accountable and if many of the complex issues that affect us all – locally, nationally, regionally and globally – are to be democratically regulated, people will have to have access to, and membership in, diverse political communities. As Jürgen Habermas has written, 'only a democratic citizenship that does not close itself off in a particularistic fashion can pave the way for a *world citizenship*. . . . State citizenship and world citizenship form a continuum whose contours, at least, are already becoming visible' (1996, pp. 514–15). There is only a historically contingent connection between the principles underpinning citizenship and the national community; as this connection weakens in a world of overlapping communities of fate, the principles of citizenship must be rearticulated and re-entrenched. Moreover, in the light of this development, the connection between patriotism and nationalism becomes easier to call into question, and a case can be built to bind patriotism to the defence of core civic and political principles – not to the nation or country for their own sake (Heater, 2002). Only national identities open to diverse solidarities, and shaped by respect for general rules and principles, can accommodate themselves successfully to the challenges of a global age.

The international community has already produced a body of common rules and standards, explored in the next three chapters, which ground this possibility, and which can be elaborated and built on in the future. In addition, the changing practices of citizenship itself are pushing in this direction. For example, a typical resident of Glasgow can participate and vote in city elections, as well as in those of Scotland, the UK and Europe. And if this is not enough, he or she can participate in the rich web of relations of global civil society. In India, a typical resident of Calcutta can participate in city, regional and state-wide elections as well as in varied transnational social movements and organizations. These complex and overlapping political relations anticipate a world increasingly defined by multiple forms of citizenship, anchored in clear and established general rules and principles.

Part III
LAW

7

Sovereignty and the Changing Structure of International Law

International political and legal change since the late nineteenth century has laid the basis of a rule-bound multilateral order. From the United Nations system to the European Union, from changes in the laws of war to the entrenchment of human rights, from the emergence of international environmental regimes to the foundation of the International Criminal Court, a legal process has been unfolding which, albeit in a slow and often halting way, has sought to reframe human activity and entrench it in law, rights and responsibilities. To take just one illustration: in the eighteenth and nineteenth centuries sovereignty meant effective power. It was not enough for the colonials to say 'first come, first served' when it came to claims to territory, for there were usually other people living in the colonies first! Instead, the principle of effective power was devised. It asserted that if you possess a territory and can demonstrate the continuous presence of your flag, then you have a right to it in international law. This claim legitimized the seizure of over half the world's territories for colonial purposes. But since 1945 sovereignty has increasingly been redefined as legitimate authority, authority based on the maintenance of human rights and democracy. This might not seem at first glance a very significant development, but it is; in the space of just fifty years the anchors have been created – from the foundation of the UN to the spread of human rights values – on which to build a more progressive multilateral future.

The foundations for this development are to be found in the actual attempts to transform the meaning of legitimate political authority from effective control to the maintenance of basic standards or values, which no political agent, whether a representative of a government or state, should, in principle, be able to abrogate. It is useful to highlight some of the legal transformations that have taken place – in the domains of war, war crimes, human rights and democratic participation, as well as the environment – which underlie this shift. In the main, these transformations have been ushered in with the approval and consent of states, but the delegation of and changes in sovereignty have, it will be seen, acquired a status and momentum of their own.

Rules of warfare and weaponry

The formation of the rules of warfare has been based on the presupposition that, while war cannot be abolished, some of its most appalling consequences, for soldiers and citizens alike, should be made illegal. The aim of these rules is to limit conduct during war to minimum standards of civilized behaviour that will be upheld by all parties to an armed conflict. While the rules of warfare are, of course, often violated, they have served in the past to provide a brake on some of the more indiscriminate acts of violence. The major multilateral conventions governing war date back to the Declaration of Paris of 1856, which sought to limit sea warfare by prohibiting privateering, and to specify the conditions under which a blockade could be said to be effective, with determinate legal consequences. Important milestones include the Geneva Convention of 1864 (revised in 1906), the Hague Conventions of 1899 and 1907, and the Geneva Conventions of 1929 and 1949 which, together, helped codify humane treatment for the wounded in the field, acceptable practices of land warfare, the rights and duties of the parties to a conflict (and of neutral states and persons), and a plethora of rules governing the treatment of prisoners and the protection of civilians. In addition to these and other regional treaties, the behaviour of belligerents is, in principle, circumscribed by elements of customary international law and by a general acknowledgement of a 'law of humanity', forbidding 'unwarranted cruelty or other actions affronting public morality' (Plano and Olton, 1988, p. 193; see Byers, 1999).

The rules of warfare form an evolving framework of regulations seeking to restrain the conduct of parties to an international armed conflict. The rules are premised on the 'dual notion that the adverse effects of war should be alleviated as much as possible (given military necessities), and that the freedom of the parties to resort to methods and means of warfare is not unlimited' (Dinstein, 1993, p. 966). These guiding orientations and the agreements to which they have given rise mark, in principle, a significant change over time in the legal direction of the modern state, for they challenge the principle of military autonomy and question national sovereignty at one of its most delicate points – the relationship between the military and the state (what it is that each can legitimately ask of the other) and the capacity of both to pursue their objectives irrespective of the consequences.

Conventions on the conduct of war have been complemented by a series of agreements on the use of different types of weapons, from the rules governing the use of dumdum bullets (the Hague Convention, 1907) and the use of submarines against merchant ships (the Paris Protocol of 1936) to a whole range of recently negotiated agreements on conventional and nuclear, chemical and biological weapons (see SIPRI, 1999). As a result, arms control and regulation have become a permanent feature of international politics. Agencies for arms control and disarmament (or sections within foreign ministries) now exist within all the world's major states, managing what has become a continuous diplomatic and regulatory process (see Held et al., 1999, pp. 123–33). Many recent agreements, moreover, have created mechanisms of verification or commitments which intrude significantly on national sovereignty and military autonomy. For example, the 1993 Chemical Weapons Convention, a near-universal disarmament treaty, creates an international inspectorate to oversee its implementation (anxiety about which filled the US Senate with complaints about 'surrendered sovereignty' (Wright, 2000)). Accordingly, it is not unreasonable to claim that the international laws of war and weapons control have shaped and helped nurture a global infrastructure of conflict

121

and armaments regulation, even though challenges to it frequently take place.

War crimes and the role of the individual

The process of the gradual delimitation of state power can be illustrated further by another strand in international legal thinking which has overturned the primacy of the state in international law, and buttressed the role of the individual, in relation to, and with responsibility for, systematic violence against others. In the first instance, by recognizing the legal status of conscientious objection, many states have acknowledged that there are clear occasions when an individual has a moral obligation beyond that of his or her obligation as a citizen of a state (see Vincent, 1992, pp. 269–92). The refusal to serve in national armies triggers a claim to a 'higher moral court' of rights and duties. Such claims are exemplified as well in the changing legal position of those who are willing to go to war. The recognition in international law of the offences of war crimes, genocide and crimes against humanity makes it clear that acquiescence to the commands of national leaders will not be considered sufficient grounds for absolving individual guilt in these cases. A turning point in this regard were the decisions taken by the international tribunals at Nuremberg and in Tokyo. It was laid down, for the first time in history, that when *international rules* that protect basic humanitarian values are in conflict with *state laws*, every individual must transgress the state laws (except where there is no room for 'moral choice', that is, when a gun is being held to someone's head) (Cassese, 1988, p. 132). Modern international law has generally endorsed the position taken by the Nuremberg and Tokyo tribunals, and has affirmed its rejection of the defence of obedience to superior orders in matters of responsibility for crimes against peace and humanity. As one commentator has noted: 'since the Nuremberg Trials, it has been acknowledged that war criminals cannot relieve themselves of criminal responsibility by citing official position or superior orders. Even obedience to explicit national legislation provides no protection against international law' (Dinstein, 1993, p. 968).

The most notable recent extension of the application of the Nuremberg principles has been the establishment of the war crimes tribunals for the former Yugoslavia (established by the UN Security Council in 1993) and for Rwanda (set up in 1994) (cf. Chinkin, 1998; Economist, 1998). The tribunal for the former Yugoslavia has issued indictments against people from all three ethnic groups in Bosnia, and has investigated war crimes in Kosovo, although it has lacked until recently the capacity to round up and arrest many of the key accused. Although neither the tribunal for Rwanda nor the tribunal for the former Yugoslavia have had the ability to detain and try more than a small fraction of those engaged in atrocities, both have taken important steps towards implementing the law governing war crimes and, thereby, reducing the credibility gap between the promises of such law, on the one hand, and the weakness of its application, on the other.

Most recently, the establishment of a permanent International Criminal Court has been designed to help close this gap in the longer term (see Crawford, 1995; Dugard, 1997; Weller, 1997). Several major hurdles remain to be overcome for its successful operation, including the continuing opposition from the United States (which fears its soldiers will be the target of politically motivated prosecutions) and dependency on individual state consent for its effectiveness (Chinkin, 1998, pp. 118–19). However, the foundation of the Court marks another significant step away from the classic regime of sovereignty as *effective power*, and towards the firm entrenchment of what I call the regime of *liberal international* sovereignty – the extension to the international sphere of the liberal concern with delimited political power and limited government.

The ground being staked out now in international legal agreements suggests that the containment of armed aggression and abuses of power can only be achieved through both the control of warfare and the prevention of the abuse of human rights. For it is only too apparent that many forms of violence perpetrated against individuals, and many forms of the abuse of power, do not take place during acts of declared war. In fact, it can be argued that the distinctions between war and peace, and between aggression and repression, are eroded by changing patterns of violence (Kaldor, 1998a, 1998b). The kinds of violence witnessed in Bosnia and Kosovo highlight the role of paramilitaries and of organized crime, and the use of parts of national armies which may no longer be under the direct control of a state. What these kinds of violence signal is that there is a very fine line between explicit formal crimes committed during acts of national war, and major attacks on the welfare and physical integrity of citizens in situations that may not involve a declaration of war by states. While many of the new forms of warfare do not fall directly under the classic rules of war, they are massive violations of international human rights. Accordingly, the rules of war and human rights law can be seen as two *complementary* forms of international rules which aim to circumscribe the proper form, scope and use of coercive power (see Kaldor, 1998a, chs 6 and 7). For all the limitations of its enforcement, these are significant changes which, when taken together, amount to a rejection of the doctrine of legitimate power as effective control, and its replacement by international rules which entrench basic humanitarian values as the criteria for demarcating the legitimate shape of power.

How do the terrorist attacks on the World Trade Center and the Pentagon fit into this pattern of legal change? A wide variety of legal instruments, dating back to 1963 (when the Convention on Offences and Certain Other Acts Committed on Board Aircraft was opened for signature), enable the international community to take action against terrorism, and bring those responsible to justice. If all the people responsible for the 9/11 attacks could be identified and apprehended, they could face prosecution in virtually any country that obtains custody of them. In particular, the widely ratified Hague Convention for the Suppression of Unlawful Seizure of Aircraft (1970) makes the hijacking of aircraft an international criminal offence. The offence constitutes grounds for extradition under any extradition treaty in force between contracting states, and applies to accomplices as well as to the hijackers themselves. In addition, the use of hijacked aircraft as lethal weapons can be interpreted as a crime against humanity under international law (although there is some legal argument about this) (Kirgis, 2001).

Frederic Kirgis has noted that the statute of the International Criminal Court defines a crime against humanity as any of several listed acts 'when committed as part of a widespread or systematic attack directed against any civilian population . . .' The acts include murder and 'other inhumane acts of a similar character intentionally causing great suffering, or serious injury to body or to mental or physical health' (Kirgis, 2001).

Changes in the law of war, in human rights law, and in other legal domains have thus placed individuals, governments and non-governmental organizations under new systems of regulation – regulation which, in principle, recasts the legal significance of state boundaries. The regime of liberal international law has reshaped the powers and the constraints on, and the rights and duties of, states.

Human rights, democracy and minority groups

At the heart of this shift is the human rights regime (see Held, 1995, ch. 5; Held et al., 1999, ch. 1). The basic elements of this regime, and the extent and scope of its coverage, are set out in boxes 1, 2 and 3. Three interrelated features of the regime are worth dwelling on: (1) the constitutive human rights agreements; (2) the role of self-determination and the democratic principle, which were central to the framework of decolonization; and (3) the recent recognition of the rights of minority groups.

In relation to (1), the human rights regime consists of overlapping global, regional and national conventions and institutions (see Donnelly, 1998; T. Evans, 1997). At the global level, human rights are firmly entrenched in the International Bill of Human Rights, the building blocks of which are the UN Declaration of Human Rights of 1948 and the Covenants on Civil and Political Rights, and on Economic, Social and Cultural Rights, which were adopted in 1966 and came into force in 1976. These were complemented in the 1980s by the Convention on the Elimination of Discrimination against Women and the Convention on the Rights of the Child. UN agencies are responsible for overseeing this system

---

Box 1   A select list of human rights initiatives and agreements

June 1945	Charter of the United Nations
June 1946	UN Commission on Human Rights
Dec. 1948	Genocide Convention/Universal Declaration of Human Rights
Nov. 1950	European Convention on Human Rights
July 1951	Convention Relating to the Status of Refugees
Dec. 1952	Convention on the Political Rights of Women
Sept. 1954	Convention on the Status of Stateless Persons
Sept. 1956	Convention Abolishing Slavery
June 1957	ILO's Convention on the Abolition of Forced Labour
Nov. 1962	Convention on Consent to Marriage
Dec. 1965	Convention on the Elimination of Racial Discrimination
Dec. 1966	International Covenants on Economic, Social and Cultural Rights/Civil and Political Rights; Optional Protocol
Nov. 1973	Convention on the Suppression of Apartheid
June 1977	Two additional protocols to the Geneva Conventions
Dec. 1979	Convention on the Elimination of all Forms of Discrimination against Women
Dec. 1984	Convention against Torture
Nov. 1989	Convention on the Rights of the Child
May 1993	International Criminal Tribunal for Ex-Yugoslavia
Nov. 1994	International Criminal Tribunal for Rwanda
July 1998	UN conference agrees treaty for a permanent International Criminal Court

Source: UN; Economist, 1998

---

and bringing persistent abuses to the attention of the UN Security Council. The UN Human Rights Commission debates reports on human rights violations (by country, theme and emergency investigations) and seeks to exert diplomatic pressure on states. The UN Human Rights Committee reviews and comments on the obligatory reports submitted by the states that have acceded to the Covenant on Civil and Political Rights (and examines individual

Box 2 Rights recognized by the International Bill of Human Rights

The right is recognized to:	Document and article[1]
Equality of rights without discrimination	D1, D2, E2, E3, C2, C3
Life	D3, C6
Liberty and security of person	D3, C9
Protection against slavery	D4, C8
Protection against torture and cruel and inhuman punishment	D5, C7
Recognition as a person before the law	D6, C16
Equal protection of the law	D7, C14, C26
Access to legal remedies for rights violations	D8, C2
Protection against arbitrary arrest or detention	D9, C9
Hearing before an independent and impartial judiciary	D10, C14
Presumption of innocence	D11, C15
Protection against ex-post-facto laws	D11, C15
Protection of privacy, family and home	D12, C17
Freedom of movement and residence	D13, C12
Seek asylum from persecution	D14
Nationality	D15
Marry and found a family	D16, E10, C23
Own property	D17
Freedom of thought, conscience and religion	D18, C18
Freedom of opinion, expression, and the press	D19, C19
Freedom of assembly and association	D20, C21, C22
Political participation	D21, C25
Social security	D22, E9
Work, under favourable conditions	D23, E6, E7
Free trade unions	D23, E8, C22
Rest and leisure	D24, E7
Food, clothing and housing	D25, E11
Health care and social services	D25, E12
Special protections for children	D25, E10, C24
Education	D26, E13, E14
Participation in cultural life	D27, E15
Self-determination	E1, C1
Humane treatment when detained or imprisoned	C10
Protection against debtor's prison	C11
Protection against arbitrary expulsion of aliens	C13
Protection against advocacy of racial or religious hatred	C20
Protection of minority culture	C27

[1] D = Universal Declaration of Human Rights; C = International Covenant on Civil and Political Rights; E = International Covenant on Economic, Social and Cultural Rights

Source: Donnelly, 1998, p. 6

Box 3   Status of ratification of the two principal international human rights treaties

Covenant on Civil and Political Rights

Countries who have not signed	47
Countries who have only signed	3
Countries party through accession or succession	86
Countries party to treaty through ratification	57
Total	193

Covenant on Economic, Social and Cultural Rights

Countries who have not signed	47
Countries who have only signed	5
Countries party through accession or succession	87
Countries party to treaty through ratification	54
Total	193

Notes

1   The United Nations Charter did not include anything more than a general reference to 'human rights and fundamental freedoms'. The Universal Declaration of Human Rights was accepted in December 1948. It was adopted by 56 countries, with eight abstentions. In 1966 the Declaration was transformed into two detailed treaties, both of which entered into force in 1976.

2   The total of 193 countries is made up of 189 UN member states and 4 non-member states. The total that is given in the treaty information published by the UN Human Rights Commission is slightly different from the above as it includes Macau as a treaty signatory separate from China. Macau is excluded here.

3   The 47 states which have not signed the Covenant on Civil and Political Rights are not the same 47 that have not signed the Covenant on Economic, Social and Cultural Rights.

4   The data are from the UN Human Rights Commission, updated 17 August 2000. See www.unhchr.ch/html/menu2/convmech.htm.

---

petitions against those states that consented to the optional protocol). In addition, the International Labour Organization is mandated, in principle, to police the area of labour and trade union rights.

Within most of the world's regions there is an equivalent legal structure and machinery. The European Convention for the Protection of Human Rights and Fundamental Freedoms (1950) is particularly significant. It was designed to take the first steps towards the 'collective enforcement', as its preamble states, of certain of the rights enumerated in the Universal Declaration. The European agreement, in allowing individual citizens to initiate proceedings against their own governments, is a most remarkable legal innovation. Although its implementation has been far from straightforward and is fraught with bureaucratic complexities, it seeks to prevent its signatories from treating their citizens as they think fit, and to empower citizens with the legal means to challenge state policies and actions which violate their basic liberties. Human rights have also been promoted in other regions of the world, notably in Africa and the Americas. The American Convention on Human Rights, which came into force in 1978, and the African (Banjul) Charter of Human and Peoples' Rights (1981) were useful steps in this regard. But perhaps as important in promoting human rights, if not more so, have been the multiplicity of political and international non-governmental organizations which have actively sought to implement these agreements and, thereby, to reshape the ordering principles of public life (see Held et al., 1999, ch. 1).

In relation to (2), there is a notable tendency in human rights agreements to entrench the notion that a legitimate state must be a state that upholds certain core democratic values (see Crawford and Marks, 1998). For instance, in Article 21 the Universal Declaration of Human Rights asserts the democratic principle along with enumerated rights as a 'common standard of achievement for all peoples and nations' (see UN, 1988, pp. 2, 5). Although this principle represented an important position to which anti-colonial movements could appeal, the word 'democracy' does not itself appear in the Declaration and the adjective 'democratic' appears only once, in Article 29. By contrast, the 1966 UN International Covenant on Civil and Political Rights (enacted in 1976) elaborates this principle in Article 25, making a number of different declarations and other instruments into a binding treaty (see UN, 1988, p. 28). According to Article 25 of the Covenant:

Every citizen shall have the right and the opportunity, without
. . . unreasonable restrictions:
(a) to take part in the conduct of public affairs, directly or through
     freely chosen representatives;
(b) to vote and to be elected at genuine periodic elections which
     shall be by universal and equal suffrage and shall be held by
     secret ballot, guaranteeing the free expression of the will of
     the electors;
(c) to have access, on general terms of equality, to public service
     in his country.

The American Convention on Human Rights, along with other
regional conventions, contains clear echoes of Article 21 of the Universal Declaration as well as of Article 25 of the Covenant on Civil
and Political Rights, while the European Convention on Human
Rights is most explicit in connecting democracy with state legitimacy, as is the statute of the Council of Europe, which makes a
commitment to democracy a condition of membership. Although
such commitments often remain fragile, they signal a new approach
to the concept of legitimate political power in international law.
    In relation to (3), the intensification of interethnic conflict since
1989 has created an urgent sense that specific minorities need
protection (renewing concerns voiced clearly during the interwar
period). In 1992 the United Nations General Assembly adopted
a Declaration on the Rights of Persons Belonging to National,
Ethnic, Religious and Linguistic Minorities. Proclaiming that states
'shall protect the existence and national, cultural, religious and
linguistic identity of minorities', the Declaration sets out rights
for members of minorities to be able 'to participate effectively
in cultural, religious, social and public life'. While the Declaration is not legally binding, it is widely regarded in the UN system and in some leading INGOs (Amnesty International, Oxfam)
as establishing a future trajectory of international legal change.
In other contexts, the impetus to secure protection for minority
rights is also apparent. Within the Council of Europe, a Charter
for Regional and Minority Languages and a Framework Convention for the Protection of National Minorities have been elaborated. Moreover, the Organization for Security and Cooperation in
Europe has adopted a series of instruments affirming minority rights

and has founded the office of High Commissioner for National Minorities to provide 'early warning' and 'early action' with respect to 'tensions involving national minority issues' (Crawford and Marks, 1998, pp. 76–7).

Changes in human rights law have placed individuals, governments and non-governmental organizations under new systems of legal regulation – regulation which, in principle, is indifferent to state boundaries. This development is a significant indicator of the distance that has been travelled from the classic, state-centric conception of sovereignty to what amounts to a new formulation for the delimitation of political power on a global basis. The regime of liberal international sovereignty entrenches powers and constraints, and rights and duties, in international law which – albeit ultimately formulated by states – go beyond the traditional conception of the proper scope and boundaries of states, and can come into conflict, and sometimes contradiction, with national laws. A new framework of good governance is emerging (Eleftheriadis, 2003). Within this framework, states may forfeit claims to sovereignty if they violate the standards and values embedded in the liberal international order. Such violations no longer become a matter of morality alone. Rather, they become a breach of a legal code, a breach that may call forth the means to challenge, prosecute and rectify it (see Habermas, 1999). To this end, a bridge is created between morality and law where, at best, only stepping stones existed before. These are transformative changes which alter the form and content of politics, nationally, regionally and globally. They signify the enlarging normative reach, extending scope and growing institutionalization of international legal rules and practices – the beginnings of a 'universal constitutional order' in which the state is no longer the only layer of legal competence to which people have transferred public powers (Crawford and Marks, 1998, p. 2; Weller, 1997, p. 45).

But a qualification needs to be registered in order to avoid misunderstanding. The regime of liberal international sovereignty should not be understood as having simply weakened the state in regional and global legal affairs. The intensification of international law and the extension of the reach of human rights do not on their own signal the demise of the state or even the erosion of its powers. For in many respects, the changes under way represent the extension of the classic liberal concern to define the proper form, scope and limits of the state in the face of the processes, opportunities and flux of civil life. In the extension of the delimitation of public powers, another illustration is offered of how states' competencies and capacities have been, and are being, reconstituted or reconfigured, as argued in chapters 4–6.

Further, states remain of the utmost importance to the protection and maintenance of the security and welfare of their citizens. For in the regime of liberal international sovereignty it is not a question of international law versus national regulation, but rather of a multiplicity of overlapping legal competencies, institutions and agencies seeking to provide the administration necessary to protect and nurture human rights. Within this framework it is not envisaged, nor is it thought desirable or feasible, that a supranational authority could provide the sole means to both articulate and enforce the new international law. At most, it is typically considered that such an authority ought to provide a set of common standards for states or substate authorities within their jurisdiction to observe, and some system of incentives or disincentives to encourage the weakest to obtain these standards (see Beetham, 1998). The resort to force in this sovereignty model is an option of last resort to be activated only in the context of a severe threat to human rights and obligations by tyrannical regimes, or by circumstances which spiral beyond the control of particular people and agents, such as the disintegration of a state.

Environmental law

The final legal domain to be examined in this chapter is the law governing the environment, wildlife and the use of natural resources. Within this sphere the subject and scope of international law embraces not just humankind as individuals but the global commons and our shared ecosystems. While attempts to regulate the trade and use of rare species date back over a hundred years, the pace of initiatives in environmental regulation has quickened since the end of the Second World War (Hurrell and Kingsbury, 1992). The first convention on the regulation of international whaling was signed in 1946, and early treaties on the international carriage of toxic substances, minor habitat protection schemes and some regulation of the international nuclear cycle were agreed in the 1950s and 1960s. However, it was only in the late 1960s and early 1970s that the extent and intensity of international environmental regulation began to increase significantly (see Held et al., 1999, ch. 8). The key moment in this regard was the 1972 Stockholm conference on the international environment sponsored by the UN Environment Programme (UNEP). This was the first occasion on which multilateral agencies and national governments gathered to consider the whole panoply of shared environmental problems and the proper scope of the response.

Throughout the 1970s and 1980s, the regulation of international waters and the control of marine pollution became extensively institutionalized with the adoption and ratification of the London Dumping Convention (1972), the MARPOL convention on ship pollution (1978), the UN Convention on the Law of the Sea (1982) and a multiplicity of regional seas agreements on cooperation and control of pollution (the Helsinki, Barcelona, Oslo and Paris conventions, as well as the UN regional seas programme). At the heart of the classic conception of sovereignty, natural resources were regarded as legitimately falling under the sovereign authority of states on the condition that whoever possessed a resource, and exercised actual control over it, secured a legal title (see Cassese, 1986, pp. 376–90). Although this principle has been extended in recent times to cover the control of resources in a variety of areas (including the continental shelf and 'economic zones' which stretch up to 200 nautical miles from coastal states), a new concept was expounded in 1967 as a means for rethinking the legal basis of the appropriation and use of resources – the 'common heritage of mankind'.

Among the key elements of this concept are the exclusion of a right of appropriation; the duty to use resources in the interest of the whole of humanity; and the duty only to explore and exploit resources for peaceful purposes. The notion of the 'common heritage' was subject to intense debate in the United Nations and elsewhere; it was, nevertheless, enshrined in two seminal treaties, the 1979 Convention on the Moon and Other Celestial Bodies and the 1982 Convention on the Law of the Sea. Introduced as a way of thinking about the impact new technologies would have on the further exploitation of natural resources – resources which were beyond national jurisdiction on the seabed or on the moon and other planets – its early advocates saw it as a basis for arguing that the vast domain of hitherto untapped resources should be developed for the benefit of all, particularly developing nations. As such, the introduction of the concept was a turning point in legal considerations, even though there was considerable argument over where and how it might be applied. It was significantly revised and qualified by the 1996 Agreement relating to the Implementation of Part XI (of the Law of the Sea).

Further significant conventions were signed in the 1980s and 1990s to combat the risks flowing from degraded resources and other environmental dangers, including the international movement of hazardous wastes (the Basel Convention in 1989), air pollution involving the emission of CFCs (the Vienna and Montreal Protocols in 1985 and 1987) as well as a range of treaties regulating transboundary acid rain in Europe and North America. Alongside these agreements, environmental issues became points of contention and the focus of regional cooperation and regulation in the EU, the Nordic Council, NAFTA, APEC, MERCOSUR and other areas.

Against the background of such developments, the impetus was established for the 1992 Rio conference (and for the Kyoto meeting in 1997). Conducted under the auspices of the UNEP, and involving negotiations between almost every member state of the UN, Rio sought to establish the most far-reaching set of global environmental agreements ever arrived at. The Rio Declaration took as its primary goal the creation of 'a new and equitable global partnership through the creation of new levels of cooperation among states, key sectors of societies and people' (UNEP, 1993, vol. 1, p. 3). Principle 7 of the Declaration demanded that states cooperate 'in a spirit of global partnership to conserve, protect and restore the health and integrity of the Earth's ecosystem'; and Principle 12 called for 'environmental measures addressing transboundary or global environmental problems' which should, 'as far as possible, be based on an international consensus' (1993, pp. 4 and 5). The results included conventions on biodiversity, climate change and greenhouse emissions, the rainforests and the establishment of international arrangements for transferring technology and capital from the North to the South for environmental programmes (see UNEP, 1993).

Rio committed all states to engage 'in a continuous and constructive dialogue', to foster 'a climate of genuine cooperation' and to achieve 'a more efficient and equitable world economy' (UNEP, 1993, p. 14; and cf. pp. 111 and 238). Traces of the concept of the 'common heritage' can be found in its many documents, as it sought to create a new sense of transborder responsibility for the global commons, and signalled the urgency of establishing a legal order based on cooperation and equity. Implementation of its many agreements has, of course, been another story. Agreement on the scope and scale of environmental threats was difficult to achieve, as was anything resembling a consensus on where the responsibility should lie for creating these and how the costs should be allocated to ameliorate them. Even where agreement was possible, international organizations have lacked the authority to ensure it is observed. Other than through moral pressure, no mechanism exists for forcing recalcitrant states into line, and the latter retain an effective veto over environmental policy through inaction and indecision. The Rio Declaration had a great deal to say about 'the new global partnership' tackling transborder problems which escape national jurisdiction, but it offered little precision on the principles of accountability and enforcement. Accordingly, while international environmental law constitutes a large and rapidly changing corpus of rules, quasi-rules and precedents which set down new directions in legal thinking, the implications of these for the balance between state power and global and regional bodies remain, to say the least, fuzzy. International environmental treaties, regimes and organizations have placed in question elements of the sovereignty of modern states – that is, their entitlement to rule exclusively within delimited borders – but it has not yet locked the drive for national self-determination and its related 'reasons of state' into a transparent, effective and accountable global framework. The limits of the liberal international order are reached.

8

Liberal International Sovereignty: Achievements and Limitations

The classic regime of sovereignty has been recast by changing processes and structures of regional and global order. States are locked into diverse, overlapping political and legal domains – which can be thought of as an emerging multilayered political system. National sovereignty and autonomy are now embedded within broader frameworks of governance and law, in which states are increasingly but one site for the exercise of political power and authority. While this is, in principle, a reversible shift, the classic regime of state sovereignty has undergone significant alteration. It is useful to rehearse the most substantial changes before reflecting on the difficulties, dilemmas and limitations of these processes.

The most substantial points can be put briefly. Sovereignty can no longer be understood in terms of the categories of untrammelled effective power. Rather, a legitimate state must increasingly be understood through the language of democracy and human rights. Legitimate authority has become linked, in moral and legal terms, with the maintenance of human rights values and democratic standards. The latter set a *limit* on the *range of acceptable diversity* among the political constitutions of states (Beitz, 1979, 1994, 1998).

States must submit, moreover, to new and intensified forms of surveillance and monitoring in the face of the increasing number of international regimes (concerned with issues as diverse as arms control and human rights abuses), international courts (from the International Court of Justice to the ICC) and supranational authorities (from the EU to the UN system). As one commentator

137

aptly put it apropos of the UN covenants on human rights, although they 'have the status of an intergovernmental treaty, once a state has ratified them it in effect acknowledges the right of a supranational body to investigate and pass judgement on its record. How a state treats its own citizens can thus no longer be regarded as a purely internal matter for the government concerned' (Beetham, 1998, pp. 61–2). The behaviour of rulers has been modified in many cases (in Kenya, Indonesia and Morocco, among other countries) by a combination of pressure and persuasion from international organizations, transnational advocacy networks, foreign donors and opposition groups (Risse, 1999). The catalogue of human rights failures is, of course, all too familiar. But the acknowledgement of this can itself be interpreted as a testimony to the extent to which the new regime of human rights has laid down, and codified, new conceptions about the proper form and limits of state action (see Rosas, 1995; Forsythe, 1991). Hence, one can speak of a transformation, albeit an incomplete and fragile transformation, of the international regime of political power.

At the beginning of the twenty-first century, the main corollaries of the classic system of sovereign law are all open to reassessment – that is, recognition of heads of state irrespective of their constitutional standing; international law's de facto approach to sovereignty; the disjuncture between considerations of appropriate rules and organizations for the shaping of domestic politics (where possible, democratic procedures, processes and institutions) and those thought applicable in the realm of realpolitik (where necessary, the forceful pursuit of 'reasons of state'); and the refusal to bestow legitimacy or confer recognition on those who forcefully challenge established national regimes or existing boundaries. Today, the legitimacy of state leadership cannot be taken for granted and, like the constitutional standing of a national polity, is subject to scrutiny and tests with respect to human rights and liberal democratic standards (Crawford and Marks, 1998, pp. 84–5). In addition, the growth of regional and global governance, with responsibility for areas of increasing transborder concern from pollution and health to trade and financial matters, has helped close the gap between the types of organization thought relevant to national and transnational life. Finally, there have been important cases where governments within settled borders (such as the Rhodesian government after its unilateral declaration of independence in 1965) have remained unrecognized by the international community while, at the same time, national liberation movements have been granted new levels of recognition or respect (for example, the African National Congress in the late 1980s during the closing stages of apartheid in South Africa). In addition, some struggles for autonomy have been accepted by significant powers, for instance the Croatian struggle for nationhood, prior to borders being redrawn and recast.

Boundaries between states are of decreasing legal and moral significance. States are no longer regarded as discrete political worlds. International standards breach boundaries in numerous ways. Within Europe the European Convention for the Protection of Human Rights and Fundamental Freedoms and the EU create new institutions and layers of law and governance which have divided political authority; any assumption that sovereignty is an indivisible, illimitable, exclusive and perpetual form of public power – entrenched within an individual state – is now defunct (Held, 1995, pp. 107–13). Within the wider international community, rules governing war, weapon systems, war crimes, human rights and the environment, among other areas, have transformed and delimited the order of states, embedding national polities in new forms and layers of accountability and governance (from particular regimes such as the Nuclear Non-Proliferation agreement to wider frameworks of regulation laid down by the UN Charter and a host of specialized agencies (see figure 8 and table 6, pp. 80–3). Accordingly, the boundaries between states, nations and societies can no longer claim the deep legal and moral significance they once had in the era of classic sovereignty; they can be judged, along with the communities they embody, by general, if not universal, standards. That is to say, they can be scrutinized and appraised in relation to standards which, in principle, apply to each person, each individual, who is held to be equally worthy of concern and respect. Concomitantly, shared membership in a political community, or spatial proximity, is not regarded as a sufficient source of moral privilege (Beitz, 1998, cf. 1979; Pogge, 1989, 1994; Barry, 1999; and see below). Elements are in place not just for a liberal but for a truly internationalist or cosmopolitan framework of global law.

The political and legal transformations of the last fifty years have gone some way towards circumscribing and delimiting political power on a regional and global basis. Nonetheless, several major difficulties remain at the core of the liberal international regime of sovereignty which create tensions, if not faultiness, at its centre. In the first instance, any assessment of the cumulative impact of the legal and political changes must, of course, acknowledge their highly differentiated character since particular types of impact – whether on the decisional, procedural, institutional or structural dimensions of a polity – are not experienced uniformly by all states and regions. From the former Yugoslavia to Afghanistan, and from the UK to the US, the extent, nature and form of the enmeshment of states in global legal and political structures clearly vary.

Secondly, while the liberal political order has gone some way towards taming the arrogance of 'princes' and 'princesses', and curbing some of their worst excesses within and outside their territories, the spreading hold of the regime of liberal international sovereignty has compounded the risks of arrogance in certain respects. This is because, in the transition from prince to prime minister or president, from unelected governors to elected governors, from the aristocratic few to the democratic many, political arrogance has been reinforced by the claim of the political elites to derive their support from that most virtuous source of power – the *demos*. Democratic princes can energetically pursue public policies – whether in security, trade, technology or welfare – because they feel, and to a degree are, mandated so to do. The border spillover effects of their policies and agendas are not foremost in their minds or a core part of their political calculations. Thus, for example, some of the most significant risks of Western industrialization and energy use have been externalized across the planet. Liberal democratic America, geared to domestic elections and vociferous interest groups, does not give great weight to the ramifications across borders of its choice of fuels, consumption levels or type of industrialization – George W. Bush's refusal after his election in 2000 to ratify the Kyoto agreement on greenhouse gas omissions being a case in point. From the location of nuclear plants, the management of toxic waste and the regulation of genetically modified foodstuffs to the harvesting of scarce resources (such as the rainforests), the regulation of trade and financial markets, and the 'hot pursuit' of terrorist networks, governments by no means simply determine what is right or appropriate for their own citizens, and national communities by no means exclusively 'programme' the actions and policies of their own governments.

Third, the problem of border spillovers or externalities is compounded by a world increasingly marked by what was referred to earlier as 'overlapping communities of fate' – where the trajectories of each and every country are more tightly entwined than ever before. While democracy remains rooted in a fixed and bounded territorial conception of political community, contemporary regional and global forces disrupt any simple correspondence between national territory, sovereignty, political space and the democratic political community. These forces enable power and resources to flow across, over and around territorial boundaries, and escape mechanisms of national democratic control. Questions about who should be accountable to whom, which socioeconomic processes should be regulated at what levels (local, national, regional, global), and on what basis, are left outside the sphere of liberal international thinking (see chapter 6).

Fourth, while many pressing policy issues, from the regulation of financial markets to the management of genetic engineering, create challenges which transcend borders, and generate new transnational constituencies, existing intergovernmental organizations are insufficient to resolve these, as discussed in part II. Decision-making in leading IGOs, for instance the World Bank and the IMF, is often skewed to dominant geopolitical and geoeconomic interests, whose primary objective has typically been to ensure flexible adjustment to the international economy – downplaying, for example, the external origins of a country's difficulties and the asymmetric rules, double standards and structural pressures of the world trading and financial systems. Moreover, even when such interests do not prevail, a crisis of legitimacy threatens these institutions. For the 'chains of delegation' from national states to multilateral rule-making bodies are too long, the basis of representation is often unclear, and the mechanisms of accountability of the technical elites themselves who run the IGOs are weak or obscure (Keohane, 1998). Agenda setting and decision procedures frequently lack transparency, key negotiations are held in secret and there is little or no wider accountability to the UN system or to any democratic forum more broadly. Problems of transparency, accountability and democracy prevail at the global level. Whether 'princes' and 'princesses' rule in cities, states or multilateral bodies, their power will remain arbitrary unless tested and redeemed through accountability chains and democratic processes which embrace all those significantly affected by them.

Fifth, serious deficiencies can, of course, be documented in the implementation and enforcement of democratic and human rights, and of international law more generally. Despite the development and consolidation of the regime of liberal international sovereignty, massive inequalities of power and in economic resources continue to grow, raising questions about the extent to which rights are entrenched in many places. The human rights agenda often has a hollow ring. There is an accelerating gap between rich and poor states, as previously noted (chapter 2). The development of regional trade and investment blocs, particularly the Triad (NAFTA, the EU and Japan), has concentrated economic transactions within and between these areas (Thompson, 2000). The Triad accounts for two-thirds to three-quarters of world economic activity, with shifting patterns of resources across each region. However, one further element of inequality is particularly apparent: a significant proportion of the world's population remains marginal to these networks, with little, if any, opportunity to enjoy in practice the liberties promised by the human rights agenda (Pogge, 1999, p. 27; see UNDP, 1997, 1999; Held and McGrew, 2002a).

Does this growing gulf in the life circumstances and life chances of the world's population highlight intrinsic limits to the liberal international order or should this disparity be traced to other phenomena – the particularization of nation-states or the inequalities of regions with their own distinctive cultural, religious and political problems? The latter are undoubtedly contributors to the disparity between the universal claims of the human rights regime and its often tragically limited impact (see Pogge, 1999; Leftwich,

2000). But one of the key causes of the gulf lies elsewhere – in the tangential impact of the liberal international order on the regulation of economic power and market mechanisms. The focus of the liberal international order is on the curtailment of the abuse of political power, not economic power. It has few, if any, systematic means to address sources of power other than the political (see Held, 1995, part 3). Hence, it is hardly a surprise that liberal democratic processes, human rights and flourishing economic inequalities exist side by side.

The implications of the above points for international law have been well summarized by Christine Chinkin when she insists that 'the capability of the international legal system to be relevant to human rights requires dislodging legal and conceptual boundaries between . . . human rights law and international economic law, between state sovereignty and transnational law, between international humanitarian law and military necessity' (1998, p. 121). The prevailing uncertainty about the meaning and implications of the regime of liberal international sovereignty is compounded by these divisions; legal uncertainty both articulates and expresses important gulfs between politics and economics (cf. Gessner, 1998).

9

The Development of Global Rules

The previous two chapters have many implications for the formation and implementation of international law, but I will focus on two broad sets of implications here: first, those concerned with security and human rights; second, those concerned with the interrelation between law, politics and economics – issues I refer to under the heading of 'the reframing of the market'.

Recasting security and law enforcement

Since 9/11 there has been a danger of a growing divergence between the American-led security agenda, on the one side, and the human rights, development and welfare agenda, on the other. The difference can be put simply by adapting Tony Blair's famous slogan on crime: 'tough on crime and tough on the causes of crime'. In global political terms this means being tough on security threats and tough on the conditions which breed them.

If one takes a narrow security agenda and ignores the social and political causes of sympathy for terrorism, then it will be harder than ever to win over the many millions who, across many countries in the Middle East and elsewhere, hold a romantic conception of the role of the 9/11 terrorists. This is not to say that Al-Qaeda or the Saddam Husseins of the world are the Robin Hoods of our age – not at all. But many perceive them in that way, and this is related to the geopolitical and social stagnation of some of the world's most vulnerable areas. It is the result of the disenchantment felt about the chances of successfully establishing peaceful ways of addressing long-held grievances. In general terms, what is required, if the tests of global social democracy are to be met in the sphere of security, is movement towards the application and extension of the rule of law in international affairs and conflict situations, and the fostering of collaboration between communities in place of violence and terror (Held and Kaldor, 2001). This requires three things of governments and international institutions.

First, there must be a commitment to the rule of law and the development of multilateral institutions – not the prosecution of war *per se*. Civilians of all faiths and nationalities need protection, wherever they live. Terrorists and all those who systematically violate the sanctity of life and human rights must be brought before an international criminal court that commands cross-national support. This does not preclude internationally sanctioned military action to arrest suspects, dismantle terrorist networks and deal with aggressive rogue states – far from it. But such action should always be understood as a robust form of international law enforcement, above all as a way of protecting civilians and bringing suspects to trial. Moreover, this type of action must scrupulously preserve both the laws of war and human rights law. In short, if justice is to be dispensed impartially, no power can act as judge, jury and executioner. What is needed is momentum towards global, not American or Russian or Chinese or British or French, justice. We must act together to sustain and strengthen a world based on common rules (Solana, 2003).

Second, a sustained effort has to be undertaken to generate new forms of global political legitimacy for international institutions involved in security and peace-making. This must include the condemnation of systematic human rights violations wherever they occur, and the establishment of new forms of political accountability. This cannot be equated with an occasional or one-off effort to create a new momentum for peace and the protection of human rights. Many parts of the world will need convincing that the UN's – not to mention the Western-based coalition's – interest in security and human rights for all peoples and regions is not just a product of short-term geopolitical or geoeconomic interests.

And, finally, there must be a head-on acknowledgement that the ethical and justice issues posed by the global polarization of wealth, income and power, and with them the huge asymmetries of life chances, cannot be left to markets to resolve alone (see chapters 1–3). Those who are poorest and most vulnerable, linked into geopolitical situations where their economic and political claims have been neglected for generations, may provide fertile ground for terrorist recruiters. The project of economic globalization has to be connected to manifest principles of social justice; the latter need to frame global market activity.

Today, the attempt to develop international law, to enhance the capacity of international institutions for peacekeeping and peace-making, and to build bridges between economic globalization and the priorities of social justice is threatened not just by the dangers posed by extensive terrorist networks, but also by some deeply misguided responses to them. These have been given particular shape by the new security agenda of the American neoconservatives and the National Security doctrine of the current American administration (published in September 2002), with its emphasis on necessary unipolarity and the unilateral and pre-emptive use of force. This doctrine, which arrogates to the United States the global role of setting standards, weighing risks, assessing threats and meting out justice, breaks with the fundamental premises of the post-1945 world order with its commitment to deterrence, stable relations among major powers and the development of multilateral institutions to address common problems (Ikenberry, 2002, pp. 44f.). It regards formerly held strategic views and diplomatic positions as, in general, obsolete.

The new doctrine of American pre-eminence has many serious implications (Hoffmann, 2003). Among these are a return to an old realist understanding of international relations as, in the last analysis, a 'war of all against all', in which states rightly pursue their national interest unencumbered by attempts to establish internationally recognized limits (self-defence, collective security) on their ambitions. But if this 'freedom' is (dangerously) granted to the US, why not also to Russia, China, India, Pakistan, North

Korea and so on? It cannot be consistently argued that all states bar one should accept limits on their self-defined goals.[1] The flaws of international law and the UN Charter can either be addressed, or taken as an excuse for further weakening international institutions and legal arrangements. In sum, there is a serious risk at present of the triumph of a narrowly focused security agenda.

Of course, terrorist crimes of the kind witnessed on 9/11 and on many occasions since (in Chechnya, Saudi Arabia, Pakistan, Morocco and elsewhere) may often be the work of the simply deranged and the fanatic and so there can be no guarantee that a more just and institutionally stable world will be a more peaceful one in all respects. But if we turn our back on this project, there is no hope of acting on the social basis of disadvantage often experienced in the poorest and most dislocated countries. Gross injustices, linked to a sense of hopelessness born of generations of neglect, feed anger and hostility. Popular support against terrorism depends on convincing people that there is a legal and peaceful way of addressing their grievances. Without this sense of confidence in public institutions and processes, the defeat of terrorism becomes a hugely difficult task, if it can be achieved at all.

A number of clear steps could be taken to help put these issues at the centre of global discussion. These include:

---

[1] It has sometimes been argued that the military intervention in Kosovo in 1999 could be the basis for exonerating the American-led attack on Iraq in 2003. It is true, of course, that in neither case was the explicit authorization of the Security Council obtained. While this was undoubtedly unfortunate, and raises difficult questions about the Kosovo intervention, the legitimacy of the latter can be argued on a number of fundamental grounds. Habermas has suggested, for example, that legitimation can be retrospectively obtained on three grounds: 'on prevention – as it seemed at the time – of an ethnic cleansing in the process of taking place, on the imperative – covered by international law – of emergency assistance holding *erga omnes* for this case, as well as on the incontrovertibly democratic and constitutional character of all the member states of the ad hoc military alliance' (2003, p. 703). These are important arguments which, together, go some way to distinguish the Kosovo and Iraq interventions. But they also serve to highlight how inadequate are the means for deliberation and decision-making about these matters at the international level. Procedural and substantive questions about the grounds for armed intervention in the affairs of another state are in urgent need of review: see below.

1   Relinking the security and human rights aspects of inter-
    national law – the two sides of international humanitarian
    (or cosmopolitan) law which, together, identify grave and
    systematic abuses of human security and well-being, and
    specify the minimum conditions required for the develop-
    ment of human agency.
2   Reforming UN Security Council procedures to improve the
    specification of – and legitimacy of – credible reasons, cred-
    ible threshold tests and credible promises in relation to armed
    intervention in the affairs of a state – the objective being to
    link these directly to a set of conditions which would consti-
    tute a severe threat to peace, and/or a threat to the minimum
    conditions for the well-being of human agency, sufficient to
    justify the use of force.
3   Recognizing the necessity to dislodge and amend the
    now outmoded 1945 geopolitical settlement as the basis
    of decision-making in the Security Council, and to extend
    representation to all regions on a fair and equal footing.

Each of these points needs clarification.

In order to reconnect the security and human rights agendas
and to bring them together into a coherent framework of law,
it would be important to hold an international or global legal
convention as a complement to, or as part of, the constitutional
convention mentioned earlier in relation to the creation of a new
global democratic assembly (see chapter 6). Rather than set out a
blueprint of what the results of such a convention should be, it is
necessary to stress the significance of a legitimate process that
would seek to combine the security and human rights sides of
international law into a global legal framework. A GIN could be
established to this end – drawing people together from around the
world, representing diverse countries, IGOs and INGOs.

One demonstrable result of such an initiative could be new
procedures at the UN to specify the set of conditions which would
constitute a threat to the peace and well-being of humankind sufficient to justify the use of force. Armed intervention in the affairs
of another country cannot always be thought of as a regressive act.
In the face of threatened or actual genocide, for example, military

intervention may, as one commentator aptly put it, be 'not merely defensible, but a compelling obligation' (Evans, 2003, p. 68). The problem is that there are no agreed international rules and regulations about armed humanitarian intervention. A global deliberative process charged with establishing such rules could examine and weigh, among other things, the serious proposals already on the public table in this regard. One such proposal comes from the Canadian-sponsored International Commission on Intervention and State Sovereignty, which presented its report to the UN Security Council in December 2001 (see www.iciss-ciise.gc.ca). The Commission turned the protracted debate about armed intervention away from the notion of a 'right to intervene' and towards the idea of a 'responsibility to protect' people in situations in which they are faced with an extreme threat, a responsibility which could trump state sovereignty if it is implicated (by an act or failure to act) in the violation of the most elemental conditions of human life. The Commission set out six principles, summarized in box 4, which it believed mark out the relevant decision-making criteria for legitimate humanitarian armed intervention.

While the principles propounded by the Commission are helpful, the question arises as to who judges when and how to apply them. The Commission was unanimous that the UN should be regarded as the principal institution for building, consolidating and using the authority of the international community, but it left the door open for other powers to be able to act if the UN failed to uphold its 'responsibility to protect' (see Evans, 2003). In so doing, the Commission risked leaving a dangerous indeterminacy about how the rule of international law can be consistently and impartially applied, and by whom. And it did not resolve satisfactorily the question of whether those who might interpret and apply the six principles should be the same as those with an interest in acting, or those who could be empowered to act, with force. Yet these issues are fundamental to any account of armed intervention in a state's affairs that hopes to command widespread acceptance. Moreover, there can be no reasonable chance of establishing a consensus in this area unless all key stakeholders – states, relevant IGOs and INGOs – are involved in the debate and come to own the proposed solutions, theoretical and institutional.

Box 4 The responsibility to protect: six principles for military intervention

The just cause threshold

(1) Military intervention for human protection purposes is an exceptional and extraordinary measure. To be warranted, there must be serious and irreparable harm occurring to human beings, or imminently likely to occur, of the following kind:
- *large scale loss of life*, actual or apprehended, with genocidal intent or not, which is the product either of deliberate state action, or state neglect or inability to act, or a failed state situation; or
- *large scale 'ethnic cleansing'*, actual or apprehended, whether carried out by killing, forced expulsion, acts of terror or rape.

The precautionary principles

(2) *Right intention:* The primary purpose of the intervention, whatever other motives intervening states may have, must be to halt or avert human suffering. Right intention is better assured with multilateral operations, clearly supported by regional opinion and the victims concerned.

(3) *Last resort:* Military intervention can only be justified when every non-military option for the prevention or peaceful resolution of the crisis has been explored, with reasonable grounds for believing lesser measures would not have succeeded.

(4) *Proportional means:* The scale, duration and intensity of the planned military intervention should be the minimum necessary to secure the defined human protection objective.

(5) *Reasonable prospects:* There must be a reasonable chance of success in halting or averting the suffering which has justified the intervention, with the consequences of action not likely to be worse than the consequences of inaction.

Right authority

(6) There is no better or more appropriate body than the United Nations Security Council to authorize military intervention for human protection purposes. The task is not to find alternatives to the Security Council as a source of authority, but to make the Security Council work better than it has.

- If the Security Council rejects a proposal or fails to deal with it in a reasonable time, alternative options are:
  - consideration of the matter by the General Assembly in Emergency Special Session under the 'Uniting for Peace' procedure; and
  - action within area of jurisdiction by regional or subregional organizations under Chapter VIII of the Charter, subject to their seeking subsequent authorization from the Security Council.
- The Security Council should take into account in all its deliberations that, if it fails to discharge its responsibility to protect in conscience-shocking situations crying out for action, concerned states may not rule out other means to meet the gravity and urgency of that situation – and that the stature and credibility of the United Nations may suffer thereby.

Source: ICISS, 2001, Synopsis

In another contribution to this pressing discussion, Anne-Marie Slaughter has argued that the proper specification of the conditions for legitimate forceful intervention depends on weighing the balance between three factors: (1) the continuing possession of weapons of mass destruction or clear and convincing evidence of attempts to gain such weapons; (2) grave and systematic human rights abuses (ethnic cleansing or genocide) sufficient to demonstrate the absence of any internal constraints on government behaviour; and (3) evidence of aggressive intent with regard to other nations (2003a). Again, this is an interesting suggestion. But how one weighs the balance of these factors, establishes a framework that can be applied to each country (and not just those who are perceived as a threat to leading interests in the West), and creates a new threshold for the legitimate use of force, is difficult to resolve and requires to be tested against the views and judgements of people who are representative of the world's regions and nations. A solution to this problem needs to be found that is not imposed from above by a select few, but rather arises from a legitimate process which has a reasonable chance of winning global political legitimacy. Only such a process, in the long run, can stipulate a new balance between international law and coercive power. Clearly, there would be much to gain from such a project, for it would take account not only of the security concerns at the heart of the recent war against Iraq, but also the fundamental human rights concerns which left many people unconvinced about the justification for the intervention in Iraq, and disturbed by its nature and extent.

Linked to such a settlement in the long run would need to be new institutional mechanisms to assess breaches of security and human rights law. No modern theory of the nature and scope of legitimate power within a state runs together the roles of judge, jury and executioner. No modern theory of legitimate power at the global level should ignore this standard. A world order based on international law and universal norms cannot be created without the separation of these powers and their distinct institutional specificity. At issue would be the creation of new global institutions which could weigh evidence in a manner that peoples around the world could find compelling and acceptable – ways which were independent of the particular interests and concerns of any one nation-state, whether powerful or humble. Under consideration in such a settlement would need to be the establishment of new forms of submission to the jurisdiction of the ICC and the International Court of Justice (ICJ), the creation of a new international human rights court, further development of regional human rights organizations, and the development of new procedures at the UN Security Council itself to test claims of serious breaches in regional or global security. The outcome could be the specification of acceptable or credible reasons for armed intervention in the affairs of another state, acceptable threshold tests for the justification for such intervention, and the establishment of credible sets of promises by any occupying power as to how it proposed to transform a country in order to meet the standards of international political legitimacy and international law (Keohane, 2003a).

But the Security Council at the centre of such deliberations could not be the same Security Council as prevails today, for this one is (as noted earlier) constituted by the geopolitical settlement of 1945. The international power structure as it was understood then was built into the UN Charter. One of the most obvious manifestations of this is the special veto power accorded to the Permanent Members of the UN Security Council. Against the backdrop of the reconfiguration of political power today, and shifting patterns of power across the world's regions, this 1945 veto power system is anachronistic. It is not just that Britain and France would not today be considered major powers deserving of such status, or that India, Japan and Brazil might be candidates for permanent inclusion, it is that the whole voting system needs to be recast to reflect better an equitable and legitimate balance of voices from across the world's regions and nations (see chapter 6; Held, 1995).

Reframing the market

Finally, it is important to return to an issue raised earlier about how to connect international legal developments with economic power and social and environmental concerns. The impact of developing 'cosmopolitan' standards, as chapters 7 and 8 argued, is highly differentiated and uneven across the world's regions. This creates moral and competitive problems for socioeconomic agents and institutions of economic governance, and generates a conundrum: how to uphold such standards and values without eroding sound economic practice and legitimate corporate interests. Outside of a cosmopolitan framework there is, I think, no escape from this conundrum.

Onora O'Neill has argued recently that in the context of political turbulence, that is, against the background of rogue states or imploding polities, corporations can find that they are 'the primary agents of justice'; that is, the primary agents with responsibility for maintaining and sustaining universal standards and virtues (2000, pp. 21–2). She holds that both states and companies can be judged by the principles and standards they claim to uphold; and that such a judgement today must be made in relation to the principles and standards which are already developing as the universal basis of action – as a result of the spread of democratic values, human rights agreements, environmental regimes and so on. This potentially lays down a tough matrix of social requirements, requirements which are at the centre of the idea of the UN's Global Compact (Ruggie, 2003). The Compact is *not* a code of conduct, but an attempt to promote core UN principles within corporate domains (see table 5, p. 70).[2]

There is much in this position to affirm: the particular culture and practices of companies matter; the difference between a responsible or rogue corporation with respect, for example, to pollution is of great significance; and the involvement of companies in the maintenance of global standards, focused, for instance, on the development of local communities, can be of marked import. None the less, corporations can find themselves extremely vulnerable to shifting competitive circumstances if they alone bear the burdens and costs of certain environmental or social standards. Business

---

[2] Through a partnership with the UN, labour organizations and INGOs, companies are encouraged to move toward and adopt 'good practices' as defined through multistakeholder dialogue about how to entrench the core UN principles. The Compact represents a 'social learning network' – operating on the premise that 'socially legitimated good practices will drive out bad ones through the power of transparency and competition' (Ruggie, 2003, p. 113).

men and women appear to object less to political regulation and social reform *per se* than to the intrusion of regulatory mechanisms that upset 'the rules of the game' in some single place or country. Stringent environmental conditions, tough equal opportunities requirements, high labour standards, more accommodating working hours, for example, may be particularly objectionable to companies if they handicap their competitive edge in relation to enterprises from areas not subject to similar constraints. Under such circumstances, companies will be all too tempted to do what they can to resist such standards or depart for more 'hospitable shores'; and this will be perfectly rational from their economic point of view.

Accordingly, if economic interaction is to be entrenched in a set of mechanisms and procedures that allow markets to flourish in the long run within the constraints of core labour, social and environmental standards, the rules of the game will have to be transformed systematically, at regional and global levels (for instance, at the level of the EU and the WTO). While corporations are already embedded in complex rule systems, these will have to be reconfigured so that companies are required to meet new standards. This target for political and economic change provides a potentially fruitful focus for both corporate interests and social movements concerned with widespread poverty, impoverished social conditions and environmental degradation. What are the institutional and procedural implications of these considerations?

The market system is highly indeterminate – often generating costly or damaging externalities with regard to health, welfare, income distribution or the environment. The 'anti-globalization' protesters are at their clearest and most articulate on these issues. These challenges can only be adequately addressed, and market economies can only function in a manner fully commensurate with core universal principles, if the market system is reframed. This should not be taken, as it all too often is, as an argument for either abandoning or undermining the market system – not at all. The market system has distinct advantages, as Hayek emphasized (1976), over all known alternative economic systems as an effective mechanism to coordinate the knowledgeable decisions of producers and consumers over extended territories. But it is an argument for restructuring – or reframing – the market itself. A bridge has to be built, as previously mentioned, between international economic law and human rights law, between commercial law and environmental law, between state sovereignty and transnational law, and between cosmopolitan principles and cosmopolitan practices (see Chinkin, 1998). Precedents exist, for instance in the Social Chapter of the Maastricht Agreement or in the attempt to attach labour and environmental conditions to the NAFTA regime, for the pursuit of this objective.

This position generates a rationale for a politics of intervention in economic life, not to control and regulate markets *per se* but to provide the basis for reforming and regulating those forms of power which compromise, disrupt or undermine fair and sustainable conditions for economic cooperation and competition – the necessary background conditions of the particular choices of human agents in a world of overlapping communities of fate. What is required is not only the firm enactment of existing human rights and environmental agreements and the clear articulation of these with the ethical codes of particular industries (where they exist or can be developed), but also the introduction of new terms of reference into the ground rules or basic laws of the free market and trade system.

At stake, ultimately, is a set of two interrelated transformations. In the first instance, this would involve extending the scope and form of the Global Compact (see chapter 3). To the extent that this led to the entrenchment of recognized universal standards in corporate practices that would be a significant step forward. But if this is to be something other than a voluntary initiative, vulnerable to being side-stepped or ignored, then it needs to be elaborated in due course into a set of codified and mandatory rules. The second set of transformations would, thus, involve the entrenchment of revised codes, rules and procedures – concerning health, child labour, trade union activity, environmental protection, stakeholder consultation and corporate governance, among other matters – in the articles of association and terms of reference of economic organizations and trading agencies. This would amount to a Global Compact with teeth. The key groups and associations of the economic domain would have to adopt, within their very *modus operandi*, a structure of rules, procedures and practices compatible with universal social requirements, if the latter are to prevail. Only by introducing new rules, standards and mechanisms of accountability throughout the global economic system, as a supplement and complement to collective agreements and measures in national and regional contexts, can an enduring settlement be created between business interests, regulatory capacity and cosmopolitan concerns (cf. Lipietz, 1992, pp. 119–24). While the advocacy of such a position clearly raises enormous political, diplomatic and technical difficulties, and would need a substantial period to pursue and, of course, implement, this is a challenge that cannot be avoided if people's equal interest in universal principles and fair practices is to be adequately protected.

There are many possible objections to such a scheme and advocacy position. Among these are pressing cultural concerns that the standards and values being projected are those of Western origin and, concomitantly, mask sectional interests – to the advantage, for example, of entrenched corporate and labour interests in the developed world. This point is often made in relation to ILO standards *vis-à-vis* child labour, freedom to join trade unions, and equal pay for men and women for work of equal value. However, this concern is, in my judgement, misplaced and hits the wrong target.

In the first instance, dissent about the value of ideas such as equal consideration of need, equal liberty and human rights is often related to the experience of Western colonialism. The way in which these ideas have been traditionally understood in the West – that is, the way in which they have been tied above all to political and civil rights, and not for example to the satisfaction of fundamental human needs – has fuelled the view that the language of liberty and democracy is the discourse of Western dominance, especially in those countries which were deeply affected by the reach of Western empires in the nineteenth and twentieth centuries. There are many good historical reasons why such language invokes scepticism. Understandable as they are, however, these reasons are insufficient to provide a well-justified critique: it is a mistake to throw out the language of equal worth and self-determination because of its contingent association with the historical configurations of

Western power. The origins of principles should not be confused with their validity (Weale, 1998).

A distinction must be made between those political discourses that obscure or underpin particular interests and power systems and those that seek explicitly to test the generalizability of claims and interests, and to render power, whether political, economic or cultural, accountable. The framework of democratic principles, human rights and cosmopolitan values is sound, preoccupied as it is with the equal liberty and development possibilities of all human beings, but it cannot be implemented plausibly without addressing the most pressing cases of economic suffering and harm. Without this commitment, the advocacy of such standards can descend into high-mindedness, which fails to pursue the socio-economic changes that are a necessary part of such an allegiance.

At a minimum, this means linking the reform packages outlined in chapters 3, 6 and 9; that is to say, linking the progressive transformation of global governance and international regulation with efforts to reduce the economic vulnerability of the poorest countries by transforming market access, eliminating unsustainable debt, reversing the outflow of net capital assets from the South to the North, and creating new finance facilities for development purposes. It means, in short, creating the basis of a new global covenant.

Part IV
THE NEW AGENDA

10

Towards a Global Covenant: Global Social Democracy

The story of our increasingly global order is not, as this book shows, a simple one. Globalization is not, and has never been, a one-dimensional phenomenon. While there has been a massive expansion of global markets which has altered the political terrain, the story of globalization is far from simply economic. Since 1945 there has been a reconnection of international law and morality, as sovereignty is no longer cast merely as effective power but increasingly as legitimate authority defined in terms of the maintenance of human rights and democratic values; a significant entrenchment of universal values concerned with the equal dignity and worth of all human beings in international rules and regulations; the establishment of complex governance systems, regional and global; and the growing recognition that the public good – whether conceived as financial stability, environmental protection or global egalitarianism – requires coordinated multilateral action if it is to be achieved in the long term. Although these developments are currently threatened by the unilateralist stance of the Bush administration, they need to be and can be built upon.

A guiding framework for elaborating on these achievements has been set down in outline in the 'global shift' of the last few decades. The transformation of sovereignty and governance is based, in particular, on values and principles which point beyond statism and nationalism. These are cosmopolitan values and principles which have been deployed to circumscribe and delimit the unacceptable face of state sovereignty. Chapters 7–9 traced out this development, indicating its achievements and limitations. The values and principles at stake – the principles of equal moral worth, equal liberty, the equal political status of all human beings, the common heritage of humankind, among others – lay the ground for a new conception of internationalism. This internationalism is defined by a commitment to cosmopolitan ethical ideals and by the attempt to entrench these in core political, social and economic institutions; it offers a framework for reshaping the nature and form of governance. At its centre is the requirement that legitimate political authority, at all levels, must uphold, and be delimited by, a commitment to the values and principles which underpin political equality, democratic politics, human rights, political and social justice, and the sound stewardship of the environment. (The cosmopolitan principles at issue are elaborated further in the Appendix.)

The contemporary phase of globalization is transforming the foundations of world order, leading away from a world based exclusively on state politics to a new and more complex form of global politics and multilayered governance. At the beginning of the twenty-first century there are good reasons for believing that the traditional international order of states cannot be restored and that the deep drivers of globalization are unlikely to be halted. Accordingly, a fundamental change in political orientation is unavoidable. Changes of outlook are clearly demarcated in the contest between the principal variants in the politics of globalization. Two leading positions – neoliberalism and that of the anti-globalization movement – are both deeply problematic. Whereas neoliberalism simply perpetuates existing economic and political systems and offers no substantial policies to deal with the problems of market failure, the radical anti-globalist position appears deeply naive about the potential for locally based action to resolve, or engage with, the governance agenda generated by the forces of globalization. How can such a politics cope with the challenges posed by overlapping communities of fate?

The same can be said, of course, about the current position of the US administration. If the US acts alone in the world, it cannot deliver core global public goods, such as free trade, financial stability and environmental sustainability, which it depends on for its overall development and prosperity. Moreover, if it acts alone it cannot achieve key domestic objectives, including leading national security goals. The fight against global terrorism requires the global pooling of intelligence, information and resources; the policing of what is left of a secure Afghanistan (Kabul) needs internationally generated resources (financial and personnel); and Iraq itself cannot be legitimately pacified and rebuilt without international cooperation, globally sourced investment and collaboration among many countries helping to supply skilled people of all kinds, from soldiers to engineers.

The alternative position is global social democracy. It seeks to build on the project of social democracy while embracing the achievements of the post-Holocaust multilateral order. Its aim is to adopt some of the values and insights of social democracy while applying them to the new global constellation of economics and politics. National social bargains, as noted in the Introduction, are insufficient to ensure an effective trade-off between the values of social solidarity, the politics of democracy and the efficiencies of the market. The challenge today, as Kofi Annan has written (1999), is to devise a similar bargain or project to underpin the new global economy. The project of global social democracy addresses this call. It is a basis for promoting the rule of international law; greater transparency, accountability and democracy in global governance; a deeper commitment to social justice; the protection and reinvention of community at diverse levels; and the transformation of the global economy into a free and fair rule-based economic order. The politics of global social democracy contains clear possibilities of dialogue between different segments of the 'pro-globalization/ anti-globalization' political spectrum, although it will, of course, be contested by opinion at the extreme ends of the spectrum.

Box 5 summarizes the project of global social democracy – the basis of a new global covenant. It does not present an all-or-nothing choice, but rather lays down a direction of change with clear points of orientation. In so doing, it draws together some of the main threads of this book, highlighting the core recommendations made in the areas of economics, politics and law. Since security considerations were confronted in both parts II and III, these have been drawn out under a separate heading in the box. Although steps taken to implement the reform programme in each

Box 5   Towards a new global covenant: global social democracy

Guiding ethical principles
Equal moral worth, equal liberty, equal political status, collective decision-making about public affairs, amelioration of urgent need, development for all, environmental sustainability

Institutional goals
Rule of law, political equality, democratic politics, global social justice, social solidarity and community, economic efficiency, global ecological balance

Priority measures
Economy
- Regulating global markets: salvaging the Doha trade negotiating round; removal of EU and US subsidies of agriculture and textiles; reforming TRIPS; expansion of the terms of reference of the Global Compact
- Promoting development: phasing in trade and financial global market integration (particularly of portfolio capital markets); expanding the negotiating capacity of developing countries at the WTO; enhancing developing country participation in international financial institutions; abolition of debt for highly indebted poor countries (HIPCs); linking debt cancellation to the funding of children's education and basic health; meeting UN aid targets of 0.7 per cent GNP; establishing new international finance facility to aid investment in poorest countries

Governance
- Reform of global governance: establishing a representative Security Council; establishment of Economic and Social Security Council to coordinate poverty reduction and global development policies; creation of environmental IGO; establishment of global issue networks on pressing social and economic problems; strengthening the negotiating capacity of developing countries; developing criteria for fair negotiations among states and non-state actors; improving cooperation among IGOs; enhanced parliamentary scrutiny of regional and international bodies

Law
- Convene an international convention to begin the process of reconnecting the security and human rights agendas through the consolidation of international humanitarian law

Security
- Developing UN Security Council principles and procedures in relation to threats to the peace and the use of armed force to intervene in the affairs of another state; enhancing monitoring capacity of the risks of, and developments concerning, humanitarian crises; implementation of existing global poverty reduction and human development commitments and policies; strengthening of arms control and arms trade regulation

Long-term measures

Economy
- Taming global markets: global antitrust authority; world financial authority; mandatory codes of conduct for MNCs
- Market correcting: mandatory global labour and environmental standards; foreign investment codes and standards
- Market promoting: privileged market access for developing countries where fledgling industries require protection; convention on global labour mobility and economic migration

Governance
- Democratization of national and suprastate governance (multilevel citizenship); global constitutional convention to explore the rules and mandates of new democratic global bodies; establishment of new international tax mechanism; creation of negotiating arenas for new priority issues (e.g. world water court); enhanced global public goods provision

Law
- Establishment of international human rights court with strong supporting regional courts; the expansion of the jurisdictions of the ICC and ICJ; the entrenchment of labour, welfare and environmental standards in the *modus operandi* of corporate practice

Security
- Establishment of permanent peace-making and peacekeeping forces; developing security and human rights threshold tests for membership in key IGOs; security, social exclusion and equity impact reviews of all global development measures

of these areas would constitute a major step forward for progressive politics, it is only by addressing the policy packages in all of them that the programme of global social democracy can ultimately be fulfilled. One of the principal political questions of our time is how such a programme can best be carried out, and how global public goods can best be provided.

A coalition of political groupings could develop to push the agenda of global social democracy further. It could comprise European countries with strong liberal and social democratic traditions; liberal groups in the US which support multilateralism and the rule of law in international affairs; developing countries struggling for freer and fairer trade rules in the world economic system; non-governmental organizations, from Amnesty International to Oxfam, campaigning for a more just, democratic and equitable world order; transnational social movements contesting the nature and form of contemporary globalization; and those economic forces that desire a more stable and managed global economy.

A complex set of parties and commitments would be needed to make a compelling coalition for global social democracy. But while it would be complex, it is not impossible to envisage. In fact, some of its core ingredients could be stipulated as follows:

- leading European powers need to commit to the creation of a multilateral order, and not a multipolar one in which they simply pursue their own state interests above all else;
- the EU must address its weak geopolitical and strategic capacity via the development of a rapid reaction force and the creation of a common European defence force;
- the US needs to acknowledge that its long-term strategic, economic and environmental interests can only be achieved collaboratively, and it must, as a matter of principle, accept the opportunities and constraints afforded by multilateral institutions and international regimes;
- developing countries, seeking major aid and overseas investments (public and private), need to accept the establishment of transparent and good governance as part of the requirements to attract investment in the infrastructure of their economies and societies;

- INGOs need to understand that, while their voices in global affairs are important, they represent particular interests which need to be articulated with, and harnessed within, wider frameworks of accountability and justice;
- IGOs utilizing and advocating greater public funding have to recognize that they are part of an international civil service delivering core public goods – and not outposts of particular nation-states or sectional interests. The confusing and conflicting mandates and jurisdictions of IGOs need to be streamlined and clarified;
- regional governance structures, while enhancing and expanding the developmental opportunities of their member states, must commit to keeping regions open for economic and diplomatic engagement with others – in short, they need to nurture open forms of regionalism;
- national governments must recognize that they are stakeholders in global problems and that ownership of these is a crucial first stage in their resolution – national and regional parliaments need to enhance their communication with, understanding of and engagement with supranational governance.

Europe could have a distinctive role in pursuing the cause of global social democracy (McGrew, 2002a). As the home of both social democracy and a historic experiment in governance beyond the state, Europe has accumulated a wealth of experience in considering institutional designs for suprastate governance. It offers novel ways of thinking about governance beyond the state which encourage a more accountable and rule-bound – as opposed to more neoliberal or unilateralist – approach to global governance. This is not to suggest that the EU should lead an anti-US coalition of transnational and international forces. On the contrary, it is crucial to recognize the complexity of US domestic politics and the existence of progressive social, political and economic forces seeking to advance a rather different kind of world order from that championed by the current neoconservatives (Nye, 2002).

While some of those who might coalesce around a movement for global social democracy would inevitably have divergent interests on a wide range of issues, there is potentially an important over-lapping sphere of concern among them for the strengthening of multilateralism, building new institutions for providing global public goods, regulating global markets, deepening accountability, protecting the environment and urgently remedying social injust-ices that kill thousands of men, women and children daily. And there is evidence that the thrust of such a coalition would resonate with people's attitudes to globalization in many parts of the world. A recent poll highlights that while many people have positive views about the broad benefits of globalization, they want a different kind of globalization from the one currently on offer: the integra-tion of economies and societies has to be balanced with the pro-tection of local traditions, with a sustainable pace of life, and with a global social safety net to help ensure equitable life chances (see Stokes, 2003; www.people-press.org).

High stakes

Over the last one hundred years political power has been reshaped and reconfigured. It has been diffused below, above and alongside the nation-state. Globalization has brought large swathes of the world's population 'closer together' in overlapping communities of fate. Yet there are, obviously enough, many reasons for pess-imism. There are storm clouds ahead. Globalization has not just integrated peoples and nations, but created new forms of antag-onism. The globalization of communications does not just make it easier to establish mutual understanding, but often highlights what it is that people do not have in common and how and why differ-ences matter. The dominant political game in the 'transnational town' remains geopolitics. Ethnic self-centredness, right-wing nation-alism and unilateralist politics are once again on the rise, and not just in the West. However, the circumstances and nature of politics have changed. Like national culture and state traditions, a vibrant internationalism and global social democracy are a cul-tural and political project, but with one difference: they are better adapted and suited to our regional and global age. Unfortunately, the arguments in support of them have yet to be fully articulated in many parts of the world; and we fail here at our peril.

It is important to return to the themes of the Preface – 9/11 and the war in Iraq – and to say what they mean in this context. One cannot accept the burden of putting accountability and justice right in one realm of life – physical security and political cooperation among defence establishments – without at the same time seeking to put it right elsewhere. If the political and the security, the social and the economic dimensions of accountability and justice are separated in the long term – as is the tendency in the global order today – the prospects of a peaceful and civil society will be bleak indeed. Popular support against terrorism, as well as against political violence and exclusionary politics of all kinds, depends on convincing people that there is a legal, responsive and specific way of addressing their grievances. For this reason, globalization without global social democracy could fail.

Against the background of 9/11, the current unilateralist stance of the US and the desperate cycle of violence in the Middle East and elsewhere, the advocacy of global social democracy may appear like an attempt to defy gravity or to walk on water! And, indeed, if it were a case of having to adopt global social democracy all at once or not at all, this would be true. But it is no more the case than was the pursuit of the modern state at the time of its founders. Over the last several decades the growth of multilateralism and the development of international law have created social democratic anchors for the world. These are the basis for the further consolidation of social democratic principles and institutions. Moreover, a coalition of political groupings could emerge to push these achievements further. Of course, how far such forces can unite around these objectives – and can overcome fierce opposition from well-entrenched geopolitical and geoeconomic interests – remains to be seen. The stakes are high, but so too are the potential gains for human security and development if the aspirations for global social democracy can be realized. One thing is clear; existing security and development policies are not working well enough and the case for a new politics and policy mix is overwhelming.

Appendix

The Basis of a New Internationalism: Cosmopolitan Principles

Clues as to what internationalism should mean today can be found in the emergent cosmopolitan values and standards, documented in part III, that characterize some leading elements of the multilateral political and legal order. What does cosmopolitan mean in this context? In the first instance, cosmopolitanism refers to those basic values that set down standards or boundaries which no agent, whether a representative of a global body, state or civil association, should be able to violate. Focused on the claims of each person as an individual or as a member of humanity as a whole, these values espouse the idea that human beings are in a fundamental sense equal, and that they deserve equal political treatment; that is, treatment based on the equal care and consideration of their agency, irrespective of the community in which they were born or brought up. After over two hundred years of nationalism and sustained nation-state formation, such values could be thought of as out of place. But such values are already enshrined in the law of war, human rights law and the statute of the ICC, among many other international rules and legal arrangements.

Second, cosmopolitanism can be taken to refer to those forms of political regulation and lawmaking that create powers, rights and constraints which go beyond the claims of nation-states and which have far-reaching consequences, in principle, for the nature and form of political power. These regulatory forms can be found in the domain between national law and international law and regulation – the space between domestic law which regulates the relations between a state and its citizens, and traditional international law which applies primarily to states and interstate relations (Eleftheriadis, 2000). This space is already filled by a plethora of legal regulation, from the legal instruments of the EU, and the international human rights regime as a global framework for promoting rights, to the diverse agreements of the arms control system and environmental regimes. Cosmopolitanism is not made up of political ideals for another age, but embedded in rule systems and institutions which have already transformed state sovereignty in distinct ways.

Yet the precise sense in which these developments constitute a form of 'cosmopolitanism' remains to be clarified, especially given that the ideas of cosmopolitanism have a long and complex history. For my purposes here, cosmopolitanism can be taken as the moral and political outlook which builds on the strengths of the liberal multilateral order, particularly its commitment to universal standards, human rights and democratic values, and which seeks to specify general principles on which all could act. These are principles which can be universally shared, and can form the basis for the protection and nurturing of each person's equal interest in the determination of the institutions which govern their lives.

Cosmopolitan values can be expressed formally, in the interests of clarification, in terms of a set of principles (see Held, 2002). Eight principles are paramount. They are the principles of:

1   equal worth and dignity;
2   active agency;
3   personal responsibility and accountability;
4   consent;
5   collective decision-making about public matters through voting procedures;
6   inclusiveness and subsidiarity;
7   avoidance of serious harm;
8   sustainability.

The meaning of these principles needs unpacking in order that their implications can be clarified for the nature and form of public life. While eight principles may seem like a daunting number, they are interrelated and together form the basis of a new internationalist orientation.

The first is that the ultimate units of moral concern are individual people, not states or other particular forms of human association. Humankind belongs to a single moral realm in which each person is equally worthy of respect and consideration (Beitz, 1994; Pogge, 1994). This notion can be referred to as the principle of individualist moral egalitarianism or, simply, egalitarian individualism. To think of people as having equal moral value is to make a general claim about the basic units of the world comprising persons as free and equal beings (Kuper, 2000). This is not to deny the significance of cultural diversity and difference – not at all – but it is to affirm that there are limits to the moral validity of particular communities – limits which recognize, and demand, that we must treat with equal respect the dignity of reason and moral choice in every human being (Nussbaum, 1996, pp. 42–3).

The second principle recognizes that, if principle 1 is to be universally recognized and accepted, then human agency cannot be understood as the mere expression of tradition or fortune; rather, human agency must be conceived as the ability to act otherwise – the ability not just to accept but to shape human community in the context of the choices of others. Active agency connotes the capacity of human beings to reason self-consciously, to be self-reflective and to be self-determining.[1] It bestows both opportunities and duties – opportunities to act (or not as the case may be), and duties to ensure that independent action does not curtail and infringe upon the life chances and opportunities of others (unless, of course, sanctioned by negotiation or consent: see below). Active agency is a capacity both to make and pursue claims and to have such claims made and pursued in relation to oneself. Each person has an equal interest in active agency or self-determination.

---

[1]   The principle of active agency does not make any assumption about the extent of self-knowledge or reflexivity. Clearly, this varies and can be shaped by both unacknowledged conditions and unintended consequences of action (see Giddens, 1984). It does, however, assume that the course of agency is a course that includes choice and that agency itself is, in essence, defined by the capacity to act otherwise.

Appendix

Principles 1 and 2 cannot be grasped fully unless supplemented by principle 3: the principle of personal responsibility and accountability. At its most basic, this principle can be understood to mean that it is inevitable that people will choose different cultural, social and economic projects and that such differences need to be recognized. People develop their skills and talents differently, and enjoy different forms of ability and specialized competency. That they fare differently, and that many of these differences arise from a voluntary choice on their part, should be welcomed and accepted (see Barry, 1998, pp. 147–9). These *prima facie* legitimate differences of choice and outcome have to be distinguished from unacceptable structures of difference reflecting conditions which prevent, or partially prevent, some from pursuing their vital needs. Actors have to be aware of, and accountable for, the consequences of actions, direct or indirect, intended or unintended, which may radically restrict or delimit the choices of others. Individuals have both personal responsibility-rights as well as personal responsibility-obligations.[2]

The fourth principle, the principle of consent, recognizes that a commitment to equal worth and equal moral value, along with active agency and personal responsibility, requires a non-coercive political process in and through which people can negotiate and pursue their public interconnections, interdependencies and life chances. Interlocking lives, projects and communities require forms of deliberation and decision-making which take account of each person's equal standing in such processes. The principle of consent constitutes the basis of non-coercive collective agreement and governance.

Principles 4 and 5 must be interpreted together. For principle 5 acknowledges that while a legitimate public decision is one that results from consent, this needs to be linked with voting at the decisive stage of collective decision-making and with the procedures

---

[2]   The obligations taken on in this context cannot, of course, all be fulfilled with the same types of initiative (personal, social or political) or at the same level (local, national or global). But whatever their mode of realization, all such efforts can be related to one common denominator: the concern to discharge obligations we take on by virtue of the claims we make for the recognition of personal responsibility-rights (cf. Raz, 1986, chs 14–15).

and mechanisms of majority rule. The consent of all is too strong a requirement of collective decision-making and would mean that minorities (even of one) could block or forestall public responses to key issues (see Held, 2002, pp. 26–7). Principle 5 recognizes the importance of inclusiveness in the process of granting consent, while interpreting this to mean that an inclusive process of participation and debate can coalesce with a decision-making procedure which allows outcomes which accrue the greatest support (Dahl, 1989).[3]

The sixth principle, which I earlier referred to as the principle of inclusiveness and subsidiarity (pp. 98, 100), seeks to clarify the fundamental criterion for drawing proper boundaries around units of collective decision-making. At its simplest, it connotes that those significantly affected by public decisions, issues or processes, should, *ceteris paribus*, have an equal opportunity, directly or indirectly through elected representatives, to influence and shape them. By significantly affected, I mean, as noted previously, that people are enmeshed in decisions and forces that have an impact on their capacity to fulfil their vital needs. According to principle 6, collective decision-making is best located when it is closest to and involves those whose life expectancy and life chances are determined by significant social processes and forces. On the other hand, this principle also recognizes that if the decisions at issue are translocal, transnational or transregional, then political associations need not only to be locally based but also to have a wider scope and framework of operation.

The seventh principle is a leading principle of social justice: the principle of the avoidance of harm and the remedying of urgent need. This is a principle for allocating priority to the most vital cases of need and, where possible, trumping other, less urgent public priorities until such a time as all human beings, de facto

[3] Minorities clearly need to be protected in this process. The rights and obligations entailed by principles 4 and 5 have to be compatible with the protection of each person's equal interest in principles 1, 2 and 3 – an interest which follows from each person's recognition as being of equal worth, with an equal capacity to act and to account for their actions. Majorities ought not to be able to impose themselves arbitrarily upon others. Principles 4 and 5 have to be understood against the background specified by the first three principles; the latter frame the basis of their operation.

and de jure, are covered by the first six principles; that is to say, until they enjoy the status of equal moral value and active agency and have the means to participate in their respective political communities and in the overlapping communities of fate which shape their needs and welfare. A social provision which falls short of the potential for active agency can be referred to as a situation of manifest harm in that the participatory potential of individuals and groups will not have been achieved; that is to say, people would not have adequate access to effectively resourced capacities which they might make use of in their particular circumstances (Sen, 1999). But even this significant shortfall in the realization of human potential should be distinguished from situations of the most pressing levels of vulnerability, defined by the most urgent need. The harm that follows from a failure to meet such needs can be denoted, as mentioned previously, as serious harm, marked as it often is by immediate, life-and-death consequences. Accordingly, if the requirements specified by the principle of avoidance of serious harm are to be met, public policy ought to be focused, in the first instance, on the prevention of such conditions; that is, on the eradication of severe harm inflicted on people 'against their will' and 'without their consent' (Barry, 1998, pp. 231, 207).

The eighth and final principle is the principle of sustainability, which specifies that all economic and social development must be consistent with the stewardship of the world's core resources – by which I mean resources which are irreplaceable and non-substitutable (Goodin, 1992, pp. 62–5, 72). Such a principle discriminates against social and economic change which disrupts global ecological balances and unnecessarily damages the choices of future generations. Sustainable development is best understood as a guiding principle, as opposed to a precise formula, since we do not know, for example, what impact future technological innovation will have on resource provision and utilization. Yet, without reference to such a principle, public policy would be made without taking account of the finite quality of many of the world's resources and the equally valid claims of future generations to well-being. Because the contemporary economic and military age is the first age to be able to take decisions not just for itself but for all future epochs, its choices must be particularly careful not to pre-empt the equal worth and active agency of future generations.

The eight principles can best be thought of as falling into three clusters. The first cluster (principles 1–3) set down the fundamental organizational features of the cosmopolitan moral universe. Its crux is that each person is a subject of equal moral concern; that each person is capable of acting autonomously with respect to the range of choices before them; and that, in deciding how to act or which institutions to create, the claims of each person affected should be taken equally into account. Personal responsibility means in this context that actors and agents have to be aware of, and accountable for, consequences of their actions, direct or indirect, intended or unintended, that may substantially restrict and delimit the opportunities of others. The second cluster (principles 4–6) forms the basis of translating individually initiated activity, or privately determined activities more broadly, into collectively agreed or collectively sanctioned frameworks of action or regulatory regimes. Public power at all levels can be conceived as legitimate to the degree to which principles 4, 5 and 6 are upheld. The final principles (7 and 8) lay down a framework for prioritizing urgent need and resource conservation. By distinguishing vital from non-vital needs, principle 7 creates an unambiguous starting point and guiding orientation for public decisions. While this 'prioritizing commitment' does not, of course, create a decision procedure to resolve all clashes of priority in politics, it clearly creates a moral framework for focusing public policy on those who are most vulnerable. By contrast, principle 8 seeks to set down a prudential orientation to help ensure that public policy is consistent with global ecological balances and that it does not destroy irreplaceable and non-substitutable resources.

These principles are not just Western principles. Certain of their elements originated in the early modern period in the West, but their validity extends much further. For these principles are the foundation of a fair, humane and decent society, of whatever religion or cultural tradition. To paraphrase the legal theorist Bruce Ackerman, there is no nation without a woman who yearns for equal rights, no society without a man who denies the need for deference, and no developing country without a person who does not wish for the minimum means of subsistence so that they may go about their everyday lives (1994, pp. 382–3). The principles are building blocks for articulating and entrenching the equal liberty of all human beings, wherever they were born or brought up. They are the basis of underwriting the autonomy of others, not of obliterating it. Their concern is with the irreducible moral status of each and every person – the acknowledgement of which links directly to the possibility of self-determination and the capacity to make independent choices.[4]

It has to be acknowledged that there is now a fundamental fissure in the Muslim world between those who want to uphold universal standards, including the standards of democracy and human rights, and reform their societies, dislodging the deep connection between religion, culture and politics, and those who are threatened by this and wish to retain and/or restore power on behalf of those who represent 'fundamentalist' ideals. The political, economic and cultural challenges posed by the globalization of (for want of a better label) 'modernity' now face the counterforce of the globalization of radical Islam. This poses many important questions, but one in particular should be stressed; that is, how far and to what extent Islam – and, of course, parts of the resurgent fundamentalist West (for instance, the religious right of the US) – has the capacity to confront its own ideologies, double standards and limitations.

It would be a mistake to think that this is simply an outsider's challenge to Islam. Islam, like the other great world religions, has incorporated a diverse body of thought and practice. In addition, it has contributed, and accommodated itself, to ideas of religious tolerance, secular political power and human rights. It is particularly in the contemporary period that radical Islamic movements have turned their back on these important historical developments and sought to deny Islam's contribution both to the Enlightenment and the formulation of universal ethical codes. There are

---

[4] It is frequently alleged that democracy itself is a Western imposition on many developing countries. Yet, as George Monbiot has recently pointed out, 'the majority of those who live in parliamentary democracies, flawed as some of them may be, live in the poor world' (2003, p. 109). Democracy has deep roots in many parts of the world; it is not an exclusively Western ideal or institution.

many good reasons for doubting the often expressed Western belief that thoughts about justice and democracy have flourished only in the West (Sen, 1996). Islam is not a unitary or explanatory category (see Halliday, 1996). Hence, the call for cosmopolitan principles speaks to a vital strain within Islam that affirms the importance of autonomy, rights and justice.

The cosmopolitan principles set out above can be thought of as the guiding ethical basis of global social democracy. They lay down some of the universal or organizing principles which delimit and govern the range of diversity and difference that ought to be found in public life. And they disclose the proper framework for the pursuit of argument, discussion and negotiation about particular spheres of value, spheres in which local, national and regional affiliations will inevitably be weighed. These are principles for an era in which political communities and states matter, but not only and exclusively. In a world where the trajectories of each and every country are tightly entwined, the partiality, one-sidedness and limitedness of 'reasons of state' need to be recognized. States are hugely important vehicles to aid the delivery of effective public regulation, equal liberty and social justice, but they should not be thought of as ontologically privileged. They can be judged by how far they deliver these public goods and how far they fail; for the history of states is, of course, marked not just by phases of corruption and bad leadership but also by the most brutal episodes. An internationalism relevant to our global age must take this as a starting point, and build an ethically sound and politically robust conception of the proper basis of political community, and of the relations among communities. Global social democracy, guided by cosmopolitan principles, would constitute a major step in this direction.

References

Ackerman, B. (1994) Political liberalism. *Journal of Political Philosophy*, 91.

Anheier, H., Glasius, M. and Kaldor, K. (eds) (2002) *Global Civil Society Yearbook, 2002*. Oxford: Oxford University Press.

Annan, K. (1999) A compact for a new century. UN document, SG/SM/6881 (31 Jan.).

Archibugi, D. (1995) From the United Nations to cosmopolitan democracy. In D. Archibugi and D. Held (eds), *Cosmopolitan Democracy: An Agenda for a New World Order*, Cambridge: Polity.

Barker, R. (1987) Fabianism. In D. Miller et al. (eds), *The Blackwell Encyclopaedia of Political Thought*, Oxford: Blackwell.

Barry, B. (1989) *Theories of Justice*. London: Harvester Wheatsheaf.

Barry, B. (1995) *Justice as Impartiality*. Oxford: Clarendon Press.

Barry, B. (1998) International society from a cosmopolitan perspective. In D. Mapel and T. Nardin (eds), *International Society: Diverse Ethical Perspectives*, Princeton: Princeton University Press.

Barry, B. (1999) Statism and nationalism: a cosmopolitan critique. In I. Shapiro and L. Brilmayer (eds), *Global Justice*, New York: New York University Press.

Beck, U. (2001) Power in the global economy. Lecture delivered at the London School of Economics and Political Science, 22 Feb.

Beetham, D. (1993) Liberal democracy and the limits of democratization. In D. Held (ed.), *Prospects for Democracy*, Cambridge: Polity.

Beetham, D. (1998) Human rights as a model for cosmopolitan democracy. In D. Archibugi, D. Held, and M. Köhler (eds), *Re-imagining Political Community: Studies in Cosmopolitan Democracy*, Cambridge: Polity.

References

Beitz, C. (1979) *Political Theory and International Relations*. Princeton: Princeton University Press.

Beitz, C. (1994) Cosmopolitan liberalism and the states system. In C. Brown (ed.), *Political Restructuring in Europe: Ethical Perspectives*, London: Routledge.

Beitz, C. (1998) Philosophy of international relations. In *Routledge Encyclopedia of Philosophy*, London: Routledge.

Bergesen, A. and Fernandez, R. (1995) Who has the most Fortune 500 firms? *Journal of World-Systems Research*, 1.

Berki, R. N. (1975) *Socialism*. London: Dent.

Bernheim, J. (1985) *Is Democracy Possible?* Cambridge: Polity.

Bhagwati, J. (1998) The capital myth: the difference in trade between widgets and dollars. *Foreign Affairs*, 77(3), May/June.

Bhagwati, J. (2002) The poor's best hope. *The Economist*, 20 June.

BIS (Bank for International Settlements) (2001) *BIS Quarterly Review* (Geneva), Dec.

Bobbio, N. (1996) *Left and Right*. Cambridge: Polity.

Bordo, D., Eichengreen, B., Klingebiel, D. and Martinez-Peria, S. (2001) Is the crisis problem growing more severe? *Economic Policy*, 32.

Bourguignon, F. and Morrisson, C. (2002) Inequality among world citizens: 1820–1992. *American Economic Review*, 92(4), Sept.

Bradshaw, Y. W. and Wallace, M. (1996) *Global Inequalities*. London: Pine Forge Press/Sage.

Budge, I. (1993) Direct democracy: setting appropriate terms of debate. In D. Held (ed.), *Prospects for Democracy*, Cambridge: Polity.

Buira, A. (2003) The governance of the International Monetary Fund. In I. Kaul et al. (eds), *Providing Global Public Goods*, Oxford: Oxford University Press.

Byers, M. (1999) *Custom, Power and the Power of Rules*. Cambridge: Cambridge University Press.

Cassese, A. (1986) *International Law in a Divided World*. Oxford: Clarendon Press.

Cassese, A. (1988) *Violence and Law in the Modern Age*. Cambridge: Polity.

Castells, M. (2000) *The Rise of the Network Society*. Oxford: Blackwell.

CEPR (2002) *Making Sense of Globalization*. London: Centre for Economic Policy Research.

Chang, H.-J. (2002) *Kicking Away the Ladder: Development Strategy in Historical Perspective*. London: Anthem.

Chasek, P. and Rajamani, L. (2003) Steps towards enhanced parity: negotiating capacity and strategies of developing countries. In I. Kaul et al. (eds), *Providing Global Public Goods*, Oxford: Oxford University Press.

Chinkin, C. (1998) International law and human rights. In T. Evans (ed.), *Human Rights Fifty Years On: A Reappraisal*, Manchester: Manchester University Press.

Clarke, I. (2001) *The Post Cold War Order*. Oxford: Oxford University Press.

Cohen, J. (1989) Deliberation and democratic legitimacy. In A. Hamlin and P. Pettit (eds), *The Good Polity*, Oxford: Blackwell.

Cohen, J. and Sabel, C. F. (1997) Directly-deliberative polyarchy. *European Law Journal*, 3(4).

Cohen, J. and Sabel, C. F. (2003) Sovereignty and solidarity: EU and US. In J. Zeitlin and D. Trubek (eds), *Governing Work and Welfare in a New Economy: European and American Experiments*, Oxford: Oxford University Press.

Conceição, P. (2003) Assessing the provision status of global public goods. In I. Kaul et al. (eds), *Providing Global Public Goods*, Oxford: Oxford University Press.

Crawford, J. (1995) Prospects for an international criminal court. In M. D. A. Freeman and R. Halson (eds), *Current Legal Problems 1995*, vol. 48, part 2, collected papers, Oxford: Oxford University Press.

Crawford, J. and Marks, S. (1998) The global democracy deficit: an essay on international law and its limits. In D. Archibugi, D. Held, and M. Köhler (eds), *Re-imagining Political Community: Studies in Cosmopolitan Democracy*, Cambridge: Polity.

Cutler, A. C. (2003) *Private Power and Global Authority*. Cambridge: Cambridge University Press.

Dahl, R. A. (1989) *Democracy and Its Critics*. New Haven: Yale University Press.

Deacon, B. (2003) Global social governance reform. In B. Deacon et al. (eds), *Global Social Governance*, Helsinki: Hakapaino Oy.

Dicken, P. (1998) *Global Shift*. London: Paul Chapman.

Dinstein, Y. (1993) Rules of war. In J. Krieger (ed.), *The Oxford Companion to Politics of the World*, Oxford: Oxford University Press.

Donnelly, J. (1998) *International Human Rights*, 2nd edn. Boulder: Westview Press.

Doyal, L. and Gough, I. (1991) *A Theory of Human Need*. London: Macmillan.

Doyle, M. (2000) A more perfect union? *Review of International Studies*, 26.

References

Dugard, J. (1997)   Obstacles in the way of an international criminal court. *Cambridge Law Journal*, 56.

Eatwell, J. and Taylor, L. (2000)   *Global Finance at Risk: The Case for International Regulation*. New York: New Press.

Economist (1998)   A survey of human rights. *The Economist*, 5 Dec.

Economist (2003)   Is the wakening giant a monster? *The Economist*, 13 Feb.

Edwards, M. and Zadek, S. (2003)   Governing the provision of global public goods: the role and legitimacy of nonstate actors. In I. Kaul et al. (eds), *Providing Global Public Goods*, Oxford: Oxford University Press.

Eleftheriadis, P. (2000)   The European constitution and cosmopolitan ideals. *Columbia Journal of European Law*, 7.

Eleftheriadis, P. (2003)   Cosmopolitan law. *European Law Journal*, 9(2).

Evans, G. (2003)   The responsibility to protect: when it's right to fight. *Progressive Politics*, 2(2).

Evans, T. (1997)   Democratization and human rights. In A. G. McGrew (ed.), *The Transformation of Democracy? Globalization and Territorial Democracy*, Cambridge: Polity.

Falk, R. (1995)   *On Humane Governance: Toward a New Global Politics*. Cambridge: Polity.

Fishkin, J. (1991)   *Democracy and Deliberation*. New Haven: Yale University Press.

Forsythe, D. P. (1991)   *The Internationalization of Human Rights*. Lexington: Lexington Books.

Gamble, A. and Payne, A. (1991)   Conclusion: the new regionalism. In A. Gamble and A. Payne (eds), *Regionalism and World Order*, London: Macmillan.

Ganghof, S. (2000)   Adjusting national tax policy to economic internationalization. In F. Scharpf and V. Schmidt (eds), *Welfare and Work in the Open Economy*, Oxford: Oxford University Press.

Garrett, G. (1998)   *Partisan Politics in the Global Economy*. New York: Cambridge University Press.

Garrett, G. (2000)   Capital mobility, exchange rates and fiscal policy in the global economy. *Review of International Political Economy*, 7, Spring.

Garrett, G. (2001)   The distributive consequences of globalization. Formerly available at www.international.ucla.edu/profile/ggarrett/papers.asp.

Garrett, G. (forthcoming)   Globalization and inequality. *Perspectives on Politics*.

References

Garrett, G. and Mitchell, D. (2001) Globalization, government spending and taxation in the OECD. *European Journal of Political Research*, 39, Mar.

Gessner, V. (1998) Globalization and legal certainty. In V. Gessner and A. C. Budak (eds), *Emerging Legal Certainty: Empirical Studies on the Globalization of Law*, Aldershot: Ashgate.

Giddens, A. (1984) *The Constitution of Society*. Cambridge: Polity.

Giddens, A. (1990) *The Consequences of Modernity*. Cambridge: Polity.

Giddens, A. (ed.) (2003) *The Progressive Manifesto*. Cambridge: Polity.

Gilpin, R. (2001) *Global Political Economy*. Princeton: Princeton University Press.

Goldblatt, D., Held, D., McGrew, A. and Perraton, J. (1997) Economic globalization and the nation-state: shifting balances of power. *Alternatives*, 22(3).

Goodin, R. (1992) *Green Political Theory*. Cambridge: Polity.

Gray, J. (1998) *False Dawn*. London: Granta.

Griffith-Jones, S. (2002) Capital flows to developing countries. Paper, UNU World Institute for Development Economics Research, Helsinki.

Griffith-Jones, S. (2003) International financial stability and market efficiency as a global public good. In I. Kaul et al. (eds), *Providing Global Public Goods*, Oxford: Oxford University Press.

Griffith-Jones, S. and Spratt, S. (2002) The pro-cyclical effects of the new Basel accord. In J. J. Teunissen (ed.), *New Challenges of Crisis Prevention*, The Hague: Fondad.

Habermas, J. (1996) *Between Facts and Norms: Contributions to a Discourse Theory of Law and Democracy*. Cambridge: Polity.

Habermas, J. (1999) Bestialität und humanität. *Die Zeit*, 18 Apr.

Habermas, J. (2003) What does the felling of the monument mean? At www.germanlawjournal.com/article.php?id-291.

Halliday, F. (1996) *Islam and the Myth of Confrontation*. London: I. B. Tauris.

Hanson, B. T. (1998) What happened to fortress Europe? External trade policy liberalization in the European Union. *International Organization*, 52(1).

Hayek, F. (1960) *The Constitution of Liberty*. London: Routledge and Kegan Paul.

Hayek, F. (1976) *The Road to Serfdom*. London: Routledge and Kegan Paul.

Heater, D. (2002) *World Citizenship*. London: Continuum.

Held, D. (1995) *Democracy and the Global Order: From the Modern State to Cosmopolitan Governance*. Cambridge: Polity.

References

Held, D. (1996) *Models of Democracy*, 2nd edn. Cambridge: Polity.

Held, D. (2002) Law of states, law of peoples: three models of sovereignty. *Legal Theory*, 8(1).

Held, D. and Kaldor, M. (2001) What hope for the future? At www.lse.ac.uk/depts/global/maryheld.htm.

Held, D. and Koenig-Archibugi, M. (eds) (2003) *Taming Globalization: Frontiers of Governance*. Cambridge: Polity.

Held, D. and McGrew, A. G. (2002a) *Globalization/Anti-Globalization*. Cambridge: Polity.

Held, D. and McGrew, A. G. (eds) (2002b) *Governing Globalization: Power, Authority and Global Governance*. Cambridge: Polity.

Held, D. and McGrew, A. G. (eds) (2003) *The Global Transformations Reader*, 2nd edn. Cambridge: Polity.

Held, D., McGrew, A. G., Goldblatt, D. and Perraton, J. (1999) *Global Transformations: Politics, Economics and Culture*. Cambridge: Polity.

Hertz, N. (2001) Decrying Wolf. *Prospect*, Aug.–Sept.

Hertz, N. (2004, forthcoming) *IOU*. London: Fourth Estate.

Hettne, B. (1998) The double movement: global market versus regionalism. In R. W. Cox (ed.), *The New Realism: Perspectives on Multilateralism and World Order*, Tokyo: United Nations University Press.

Hill, T. (1987) The importance of autonomy. In E. Kittay and D. Meyers (eds), *Women and Moral Theory*, Totowa: Roman and Allanheld.

Hirst, P. (1997) The global economy: myths and realities. *International Affairs*, 73(3), July.

Hirst, P. and Thompson, G. (1999) *Globalization in Question*, 2nd edn. Cambridge: Polity.

Hirst, P. and Thompson, G. (2002) The future of globalization. *Cooperation and Conflict*, 37(3).

HM Treasury (2003) *International Finance Facility*. London: Stationery Office.

Hoffmann, S. (2003) America goes backward. *New York Review of Books*, 12 June.

Houghton, J. (2003) Global warming is now a weapon of mass destruction. *Guardian*, 28 July, p. 14.

Hurrell, A. and Kingsbury, B. (eds) (1992) *The International Politics of the Environment*. Oxford: Oxford University Press.

Hutton, W. (2002) *The World We're In*. London: Little, Brown.

ICISS (International Commission on Intervention and State Sovereignty) (2001) *The Responsibility to Protect*. Available on www.iciss-ciise.gc.ca.

References

Ikenberry, J. (2002)   America's imperial ambition. *Foreign Affairs*, Sept.–Oct.

Jayasuriya, K. (1999)   Globalization, law and the transformation of sovereignty: the emergence of global regulatory governance. *Indiana Journal of Global Legal Studies*, 6(2).

Kagan, R. (2003)   *Paradise and Power: America and Europe in the New World Order*. London: Atlantic Books.

Kaldor, M. (1998a)   *New and Old Wars*. Cambridge: Polity.

Kaldor, M. (1998b)   Reconceptualizing organized violence. In D. Archibugi et al. (eds), *Re-imagining Political Community*, Cambridge: Polity.

Kaldor, M. (2003)   *Global Civil Society*. Cambridge: Polity.

Kaul, I., Grunberg, I. and Stern, M. (eds) (1999)   *Global Public Goods: International Cooperation in the Twenty-First Century*. Oxford: Oxford University Press.

Kaul, I., Conceição, P., Goulven, K. and Mendoza, R. (eds) (2003)   *Providing Global Public Goods*. Oxford: Oxford University Press.

Kay, J. (2003a)   *The Truth about Markets*. London: Allen Lane.

Kay, J. (2003b)   The truth about markets, *Progressive Politics*, 2(2).

Kelly, P. (2002)   Ideas and policy agendas in contemporary politics. In P. Dunleavy et al. (eds), *Developments in British Politics 7*, London: Palgrave.

Keohane, R. O. (1998)   International institutions: can interdependence work? *Foreign Policy*, Spring.

Keohane, R. O. (2003a)   A credible promise to the United Nations. *Financial Times*, 31 Mar.

Keohane, R. O. (2003b)   Global governance and democratic accountability. In D. Held and M. Koenig-Archibugi (eds), *Taming Globalization*, Cambridge: Polity.

Keohane, R. O. and Nye, J. S. (2000)   Globalization: what's new? what's not (and so what?). *Foreign Policy*, Spring.

Kirgis, F. L. (2001)   Terrorist attacks on the World Trade Center and the Pentagon. At www.asil.org/insights/insigh77.htm.

Koenig-Archibugi, M. (2002)   Mapping global governance. In D. Held and A. McGrew (eds), *Governing Globalization: Power, Authority and Global Governance*, Cambridge: Polity.

Kuper, A. (2000)   Rawlsian global justice: beyond *The Law of Peoples* to a cosmopolitan law of persons. *Political Theory*, 28.

Leftwich, A. (2000)   *States of Development*. Cambridge: Polity.

Legrain, P. (2002)   *The Open World*. London: Abacus.

References

Lichtheim, G. (1970)   *A Short History of Socialism*. London: Weidenfeld and Nicolson.

Lijphart, A. (1999)   *Patterns of Democracy*. New Haven: Yale University Press.

Lipietz, A. (1992)   *Towards a New Economic Order*. Cambridge: Polity.

McGrew, A. G. (1992)   Conceptualizing global politics. In A. G. McGrew et al., *Global Politics*, Cambridge: Polity.

McGrew, A. (2002a)   Between two worlds: Europe in a globalizing era. *Government and Opposition*, 37(3), Summer.

McGrew, A. G. (2002b)   Liberal internationalism: between realism and cosmopolitanism. In D. Held and A. G. McGrew (eds), *Governing Globalization*, Cambridge: Polity.

Maddison, A. (2001)   *The World Economy: A Millennial Perspective*. Paris: OECD Development Studies Centre.

Mathews J. (2003)   Power shift. In D. Held and A. McGrew (eds), *The Global Transformation Reader*, Cambridge: Polity.

Mendoza, R. V. (2003)   The multilateral trade regime. In I. Kaul et al. (eds), *Providing Global Public Goods*, Oxford: Oxford University Press.

Milanovic, B. (2003)   Two faces of globalization: against globalization as we know it. *World Development*, 31(4).

Monbiot, G. (2003)   *The Age of Consent*. London: Flamingo.

Moore, M. (2003)   *A World without Walls*. Cambridge: Cambridge University Press.

Mosley, P. (2000)   Globalisation, economic policy and convergence. *World Economy*, 23(5).

Murphy, C. N. (2000)   Global governance: poorly done and poorly understood. *International Affairs*, 76(4).

Neunreither, K. (1993)   Subsidiarity as a guiding principle for European Community activities. *Government and Opposition*, 28(2).

Norris, P. (2000)   Global governance and cosmopolitan citizens. In J. S. Nye and J. D. Donahue (eds), *Governance in a Globalizing World*, Washington DC: Brookings Institution Press.

Nussbaum, M. C. (1996)   Kant and cosmopolitanism. In J. Bohman and M. Lutz-Bachmann (eds), *Perpetual Peace: Essays on Kant's Cosmopolitan Ideal*, Cambridge, Mass: MIT Press.

Nye, J. S. (1990)   *Bound to Lead*. New York: Basic Books.

Nye, J. S. (2002)   *The Paradox of American Power*. Oxford: Oxford University Press.

Ohmae, K. (1990)   *The Borderless World*. London: Collins.

O'Neill, O. (2000)   Agents of justice. In T. W. Pogge (ed.), *Global Justice*, Oxford: Blackwell.

Oxfam (2002) *Rigged Rules and Double Standards.* Oxford: Oxfam.

Payne, A. (2003) Globalization and modes of regionalist governance. In D. Held and A. G. McGrew (eds), *The Global Transformations Reader*, Cambridge: Polity.

Perraton, J., Goldblatt, D., Held, D. and McGrew, A. (1997) The globalization of economic activity. *New Political Economy*, 2, Spring.

Phillips, A. (1993) Must feminists give up on liberal democracy? In D. Held (ed.), *Prospects for Democracy*, Cambridge: Polity.

Plano, J. C. and Olton, R. (1988) *The International Relations Dictionary.* Santa Barbara: ABC Clio.

Pogge, T. W. (1989) *Realizing Rawls.* Ithaca: Cornell University Press.

Pogge, T. W. (1994) Cosmopolitanism and sovereignty. In C. Brown (ed.), *Political Restructuring in Europe: Ethical Perspectives*, London: Routledge.

Pogge, T. W. (1999) Economic justice and national borders. *Revision*, 22(2).

Raustiala, K. (1997) States, NGOs, and environmental institutions. *International Studies Quarterly*, 41(4).

Raz, J. (1986) *The Morality of Freedom.* Oxford: Oxford University Press.

Reddy, S. J. and Pogge, T. W. (2003) How *not* to count the poor. At www.socialanalysis.org.

Reinicke, W. (1999) The other world wide web: global public policy networks. *Foreign Policy*, Winter.

Rischard, J.-F. (2002) *High Noon.* New York: Basic Books.

Risse, T. (1999) International norms and domestic change. *Politics and Society*, 27(4).

Rodrik, D. (1997) *Has Globalization Gone Too Far?* Washington DC: Institute for International Economics.

Rodrik, D. (2001) The global governance of trade as if development really mattered. At www.undp.org/bdp.

Rodrik, D. (2003) Free trade optimism. *Foreign Affairs*, May/June.

Rosas, A. (1995) State sovereignty and human rights: towards a global constitutional project. In D. Beetham (ed.), *Politics and Human Rights*, Oxford: Blackwell.

Rosenau, J. N. (2002) Governance in a new global order. In D. Held and A. G. McGrew (eds), *Governing Globalization*, Cambridge: Polity.

Rouleau, E. (2002) Trouble in the kingdom. *Foreign Affairs*, July/Aug.

Roy, S. (2003) What do anti-global protestors want exactly? *Global Agenda*.

References

Ruggie, J. (1982) International regimes, transactions and change: embedded liberalism in the postwar economic order. *International Organization*, 36, Spring.

Ruggie, J. (1993) Territoriality and beyond. *International Organization*, 41(1).

Ruggie, J. (2003) Taking embedded liberalism global: the corporate connection. In D. Held and M. Koenig-Archibugi (eds), *Taming Globalization*, Cambridge: Polity.

Rundra, N. (2002) Globalization and the decline of the welfare state in less-developed countries. *International Organization*, 56(2).

Sassen, S. (1996) *Losing Control? Sovereignty in an Age of Globalization*. New York: Columbia University Press.

Saward, M. (2000) A critique of Held. In B. Holden (ed.), *Global Democracy*, London: Routledge.

Sen, A. (1985) The moral standing of the market. *Social Philosophy and Policy*, 2(2).

Sen, A. (1996) Humanity and citizenship. In J. Cohen (ed.), *For Love of Country: Debating the Limits of Patriotism*, Boston: Beacon.

Sen, A. (1999) *Development as Freedom*. Oxford: Oxford University Press.

SIPRI (1999) *SIPRI Yearbook 1999: Armaments, Disarmament and International Security*. Oxford: Oxford University Press.

Slaughter, A.-M. (2003a) A chance to reshape the UN. *Washington Post*, 13 Apr.

Slaughter, A.-M. (2003b) Governing the global economy through government networks. In D. Held and A. G. McGrew (eds), *The Global Transformations Reader*, Cambridge: Polity.

Solana, J. (2003) The future of transatlantic relations. *Progressive Politics*, 2(2).

Steans, J. (2002) Global governance: a feminist perspective. In D. Held and A. G. McGrew (eds), *Governing Globalization*, Cambridge: Polity.

Stiglitz, J. (1999) Knowledge as a global public good. In I. Kaul, I. Grunberg and M. A. Stern (eds), *Global Public Goods*, Oxford: Oxford University Press.

Stiglitz, J. (2002) *Globalization and its Discontents*. London: Allen Lane.

Stiglitz, J. (2003a) *The Roaring Nineties: Seeds of Destruction*. London: Allen Lane.

Stiglitz, J. (2003b) Trade imbalances. *Guardian*, 15 Aug.

Stokes, B. (2003) Global is better. *National Journal*, 6(7).

Strange, S. (1996) *The Retreat of the State*. Cambridge: Cambridge University Press.

Swank, D. (2001) Mobile capital, democratic institutions, and the public economy in advanced industrial societies. *Journal of Comparative Policy Analysis: Research and Practice*, 3.

Swank, D. (2002a) *Global Capital, Political Institutions, and Policy Change in Developed Welfare States*. Cambridge: Cambridge University Press.

Swank, D. (2002b) Tax policy in an era of internationalization: an assessment of a conditional diffusion model of the spread of neo-liberalism. Paper, Department of Political Science, Marquette University, Milwaukee.

Teubner, G. (ed.) (1997) *Global Law without a State*. Aldershot: Dartmouth.

Thompson, G. (2000) Economic globalization? In D. Held (ed.), *A Globalizing World? Culture, Economics and Politics*, London: Routledge.

UIA (Union of International Associations) (2002) *Yearbook of International Organizations 2001/2002*, vol. 1B (Int–Z). Munich: K. G. Saur.

UN (1988) *Human Rights: A Compilation of International Instruments*. New York: United Nations.

UNCTAD (1996) *World Investment Report 1996: Investment, Trade and International Policy Arrangements*. New York: United Nations.

UNCTAD (1997) *World Investment Report 1997: Transnational Corporations, Market Structure and Competition Policy*. New York: United Nations.

UNCTAD (1998a) *The Least Developed Countries 1998*. Geneva: UN Conference on Trade and Development.

UNCTAD (1998b) *Trade and Development Report 1998*. Geneva: UN Conference on Trade and Development.

UNCTAD (2001a) *Handbook of Statistics 2001*. Geneva: UN Conference on Trade and Development.

UNCTAD (2001b) *World Investment Report 2001*. Geneva: UN Conference on Trade and Development.

UNCTAD (2002a) *Handbook of Statistics 2002*. Geneva: UN Conference on Trade and Development.

UNCTAD (2002b) *Trade and Development Report 2002*. Geneva: UN Conference on Trade and Development.

UNCTC (1983) *Transnational Corporations in World Development: Third Survey*. New York: United Nations.

UNDP (1997) *Human Development Report 1997*. New York: Oxford University Press.

References

UNDP (1998)   *Globalization and Liberalization.* New York: Oxford University Press.

UNDP (1999)   *Globalization with a Human Face: Human Development Report 1999.* New York: Oxford University Press.

UNDP (2001)   *Human Development Report: Making Technology Work for Human Development.* New York: Oxford University Press.

UNDP (2002)   *Human Development Report 2002: Deepening Democracy in a Fragmented World.* New York: Oxford University Press.

UNEP (1993)   *Report of the United Nations Conference on Environment and Development.* 3 vols, New York: United Nations.

Vernon, R. (1998)   *In the Hurricane's Eye: The Troubled Prospects of Multinational Enterprises.* Cambridge, Mass.: Harvard University Press.

Vincent, J. (1992)   Modernity and universal human rights. In A. G. McGrew et al., *Global Politics*, Cambridge: Polity.

Wade, R. (2001) The rising inequality of world income distribution. *Finance and Development*, Dec.

Wade, R. (2003)   The disturbing rise in poverty and inequality. In D. Held and M. Koenig-Archibugi (eds), *Taming Globalization*, Cambridge: Polity.

Wallace, W. (1999)   The sharing of sovereignty: the European paradox. *Political Studies*, 47(3), special issue.

Weale, A. (1998)   From contracts to pluralism? In P. Kelly (ed.), *Impartiality, Neutrality and Justice: Re-reading Brian Barry's Justice as Impartiality*, Edinburgh: Edinburgh University Press.

Weiss, L. (1998)   *The Myth of the Powerless State.* Ithaca: Cornell University Press.

Weller, M. (1997)   The reality of the emerging universal constitutional order: putting the pieces together. *Cambridge Review of International Studies*, Winter/Spring.

Whelan, F. (1983)   Prologue: democratic theory and the boundary problem. In J. R. Pennock and R. W. Chapman (eds), *Nomos XXV: Liberal Democracy*, New York and London: New York University Press.

Williamson, J. (1990)   *Latin American Adjustment: How Much has Happened?* Washington, DC: Institute for International Economics.

Williamson, J. (1993)   Democracy and the 'Washington consensus'. *World Development*, 21(8).

World Bank (2000)   *World Development Indicators.* Washington DC: World Bank.

References

World Bank (2001)   *Poverty in the Age of Globalization.* Washington DC: World Bank.

World Bank (2002)   *Global Economic Prospects 2002.* Washington DC: World Bank.

Wright, R. (2000)   Continental drift: world government is caring. *New Republic*, 25 Jan.

Index

Index

Index

United States
  Americanization and globalization
    4
  and economic globalization 28, 29
  foreign direct investment 43
  and global public goods 162
  and global social democracy 166,
    169
  and the International Criminal
    Court 123
  and the Iraq war 86
  and liberal international
    sovereignty 140–1
  and the military 86
  religious right 177
  security project xiii–xiv, 146–7,
    162–3
  and the war on terrorism 89–90,
    163
  and the Washington consensus
    xiv–xv

Wade, Robert 51
war crimes
  international law and the role of
    the individual 122–5
  and liberal international
    sovereignty 139
warfare and weaponry
  and the development of global
    rules 151
  ICISS six principles for military
    intervention 150
  and international law 120–2
  and liberal international
    sovereignty 139
Washington consensus xiv–xv, 16,
    55–6

welfare institutions, and globalization
    4–5
women
  and global inequalities 37
  and the UN Millennium
    Development Goals 64
World Bank
  and anti-globalization protests 2
  and global financial governance
    66, 68
  and global politics 9, 77
  health and social policies 94
  and liberal international
    sovereignty 141
  and social democratic
    multilateralism 112
  and trade and financial
    liberalization 52
WTO (World Trade Organization)
  and developing countries 9,
    60–1
  Doha round 57, 59, 60
  and economic globalization 29
  establishment of a social chapter
    61
  and global civil society 10
  and intellectual property rights
    60
  and interagency cooperation 95
  and political globalization 77, 79,
    87
  and social democratic
    multilateralism 112

young people, attitudes to
    globalization 92–3
Yugoslavia (former), war crimes
    tribunal 123